Understanding Sikhism

Satwant Kaur Rait

with Inderjit Bhogal

Plug and Tap

Copyright Satwant Kaur Rait

First published in 2010 by Plug and Tap,
16 Sycamore Business Park, Copt Hewick, Ripon HG4 5DF
www.plugandtap.co.uk

All rights reserved. No part of this publication may be reproduced, stored in a retrieval system or transmitted, in any form or by any means, electronical, mechanical, photocopying or otherwise, without the prior permission of the publisher, Plug and Tap.

The Author has asserted their rights under the Copyright, Designs and Patents Act 1988 to be identified as the Author of this Work.

A catalogue record for this book is available from the British Library

ISBN 978-0-9562120-4-7

Printed in Great Britain by the MPG Books Group, Bodmin and King's Lynn

Contents

Foreword

Introduction   i-iv

Research Methods   v-vi

Acknowledgement   vii

Chapter 1   **Background to Sikhism**   1-14
Sikhs and who they are
Origin of Sikhism
Sikh identity – The five K's
Sikh ethics
    Kirt karna
    Wand chhakna
    Naam japna
Core values
    Seva
    Equality
    Other beliefs
Sikh place of worship – *Gurdwara*
Sikh denominations and saint preachers
    Namdharis
    Nirankaris
    Radhasoamis
    Saint preachers
Summary

Chapter 2   **The Holy Scripture of the Sikhs**   15-20
Guru Granth Sahib
Summary

Chapter 3   **The Concept of God in Sikhism**   21-26
The concept of God in Sikhism
The gender of God in Sikhism
The place of *Gurus* in Sikhism
Summary

Chapter 4   **Origin of the Universe, Environment and**
                Ecology in Sikhism   27-30
Origin of the Universe
Environment and ecology in Sikhism
Summary

Chapter 5	**Equality and Sikhism**
	Equality
	    Caste inequalities
	    Economic (class or social status) inequalities
	    Gender inequality
	Sikh ideology and the status of women
	    Women in Sikh religion and religious practices
	    Socio-religious traditions
	Sikh attitude towards other religions
	Summary
		31-40

Chapter 6	**Family Life**
	Marriage
	    Dowry
	    Divorce
	    Family planning
	Euthanasia or mercy killing
	Summary
		41-46

Chapter 7	**Sikh Ceremonies and Festivals**
	Sikh Ceremonies
	    Birth
	    Marriage
	    Death
	Sikh religious celebrations
	    Sikh gurpurabs
	    Sikh festivals
	Summary
		47-54

Chapter 8	**Sikh Behaviour and the Sikh Way of Life**
	Background
	    Diet
	    Dress
	    Music
	    Other rituals
	        Worshipping local shrines and deities
	        Pilgrimage
	Sikh greetings
	Summary
		55-60

Chapter 9	**'Roots and Routes' an Interfaith Dialogue**	61-70
Chapter 10	**Conclusion**	71-76
Appendix 1	**Contributions of Sikh *Gurus***	77-80
Appendix 2	**Glossary**	81-90
Bibliography		91-92
Index		93-98

To
Asha Gracie, Priya,
Sacha and Rohan

Foreword

It is a particular pleasure for us to write this foreword to 'Understanding Sikhism' by our colleague on the Yorkshire and Humber Faiths Forum, Satwant Rait.

Simply, here in this book we have the distilled wisdom of Satwant whose life work it has been to talk with others about her faith and to confront all the barriers where there seem to be misunderstanding and fear. From this book we can see there are ways forward where mutual understanding can come about and where we can afresh share our understanding of what God has done across these barriers.

This educational book written in an accessible language gives an insight of Sikh values, concepts and spirituality. Inderjit Bhogal's Sikh-Christian perspective provides a helpful model for interfaith dialogue.

This most helpful book will be appreciated by all who want to be better informed about their Sikh neighbours and friends.

Tony Robinson Chair of YHFF

Sadja Shah Vice Chair of YHFF

Introduction

This is a basic book written in an easy to read and simple to understand language avoiding jargon intended to give a better understanding of Sikhism to young adults of Sikh and other backgrounds. It is an attempt to simplify Sikh religious teachings for easy comprehension but meant for advanced knowledge. The author has tried her best to explain words or terminology which have no easy interpretation in theology. It will prove a useful source material for teachers and a base for trainers to prepare relevant models for their training courses. The author's own experience of living in this country with Sikhs and the indigenous population made her realise that there is still a widespread lack of awareness about Sikhs and the Sikh faith - the faith with the fourth largest number of adherents in this country. Her growing concern is for the younger generation of Sikhs and misconception and stereotyping about the Sikh identity. The author's observations of the incidents which her son had to go through in his school and later at university and her friend's experience of different stereotypes made her more determined to write this book.

Understanding diverse faiths is becoming increasingly important as it helps to know the ways in which people's faith traditions may impact on their public as well as their private lives. There is an increasing recognition in Government circles that faith plays a central role in modern multi-faith, multi-ethnic, multicultural Britain, and affects everyone. This is seen in the Government's commitment to consultation with faith communities, and grants being allocated towards the creation of national and regional faiths forums and capacity building in faith communities. Faith communities are growing in numbers and with this their requirements and contributions are becoming visible and drawing the attention of policy makers and those responsible for delivering services to communities. It is important for policy makers and those delivering services at all levels to understand the basics of different faiths in order to address the needs of different faith communities effectively.

Britain has become multi-faith and multicultural. Most Britons enjoy equality in worshipping and celebrating their religious traditions. Religious and faith communities celebrate the important rites surrounding birth and naming, initiation into faith communities, marriage, dying, death and funerals. They also observe their traditional religious festivals. Most people want to retain and educate their children in the faith they are born in. According to the 2001 National Census, over 70% of the UK population identified themselves as belonging to a religious community. This leads to not only building worship centres, and education at home, but also faith-related education provided by educational institutions at all levels. Religious education will help individuals in acquiring knowledge of their own religion and also other world religions thus creating an understanding of each other's religious values contributing to community cohesion.

It is all too easy to exclude people from particular faith backgrounds, through ignorance, indifference and misunderstanding. This exclusion contributes to an environment in which discrimination thrives. Communities thrive and prosper through harmonious existence and this can only be created by integration. Integration requires understanding and respect for others. Understanding comes with knowledge and awareness. Written material and media are the two main sources of knowledge and raising awareness. Social interaction is another medium which creates friendship and understanding. Research has shown that there is very little social interaction between black and white communities. In these circumstances, the teachings and practices of the UK's faith communities have much to contribute towards better mutual understanding and fuller community cohesion.

Religious communities and organisations have struggled for decades to acquire legal protection. For example, the Road Traffic Act 1972 made the wearing of crash-helmets on motorbikes compulsory, but this discriminated against Sikh men for whom wearing a turban is a religious requirement, and it wasn't until the Road Traffic Act 1988 – 16 years later – that they were granted an appropriate exemption. A similar provision now exempts them from the requirement, laid down in the Employment Act 1989, for hard hats to be worn on construction sites. Both Sikhs and Jews eventually acquired protection from religious discrimination under the existing legislation, because the courts came to regard them as distinct races. However, the religious communities that could not be identified with particular racial groups were not afforded such protection.

The legislations in the past (Race Relations Acts) were the outcome of people's experiences uncovering a huge amount of discrimination evident not only in people's personal opinions and attitudes, but in the public spheres of education, employment and the media, and an overwhelming desire of faith communities and organisations to see appropriate legislation enacted to protect their members. Recognising the need for legislation specifically designed to target religious discrimination, the UK Government was active in negotiating a new common legal framework for the whole European Union. In line with EU agreements, the Government has produced new laws for the UK, called the Employment Equality Regulations (Religion or Belief) 2003 which came into force in December of that year. These cover direct and indirect discrimination, harassment and victimisation in the workplace, in relations among employers and employees. It is important to note that the Employment Equality Regulations do not cover delivery of goods, facilities and services to the public, nor public access to premises. The new Equality Bill will consolidate and simplify existing discrimination legislation. It will not only apply to race, disability and gender but also to age, gender reassignment, religion and belief and sexual orientation. It will require public bodies to consider how their policies, programmes and services affect different disadvantaged groups in the community. The Duty will also require public bodies to tackle discrimination and promote equality through their purchasing functions. The new Equality Bill will provide a strong legal framework. It will become law after being debated by Parliament in about autumn 2010.

After the attacks of 11 September 2001, the Government brought forward the Anti-Terrorism, Crime and Security Bill, containing a clause to extend the existing provisions on incitement to racial hatred and to cover incitement to religious hatred. The failure of Lord Avebury's Religious Offences Bill in 2002 led to the appointment of a Select Committee to look into the whole law relating to religious offences. There were no specific recommendations from the Committee, but in 2004 the Government confirmed its intention to treat incitement to religious hatred as an offence. The Racial and Religious Hatred Act 2006 creates an offence of inciting or 'stirring up' hatred against a person on the grounds of their religion. A significant amendment limits the legislation to "A person who uses threatening words or behaviour, or displays any written material which is threatening... if he intends thereby to stir up religious hatred" specifically removing the concept of abusing and insulting religion and religious people (to the relief of some comedians and satirists), and positively requiring the intention of stirring up religious hatred rather than just the possibility.

It is a common knowledge that Sikhs are often mistaken for Muslims. This is evident from the aftermath incidents of the attack of 11 September 2001, when some Sikhs were murdered and attacked in America and some other countries because of the mistaken identity. Such incidents signal the importance and necessity of better awareness. There is no denying the fact that numbers of books are available on Sikhism and Sikh religious traditions but there is a lack of topical material written in clear, concise and simple language.

This book deals with the basic knowledge of Sikhism. There is a growing tendency to use the word *Sikhi* in the Sikh circles rather than Sikhism thinking that this religion is not an 'ism' but a way of life. I chose to use the word Sikhism intentionally as this word is popularly and widely known in theology. The word Sikh is used for any person adhering to Sikh teachings whereas the words '*amritdhari* and '*Khalsa*' are used for initiated Sikhs. The book is divided in chapters based on the questions frequently asked and discussed in religious studies and interfaith dialogue. A summary is attached to each and every chapter for quick reference. The author tried her best to express the Sikh faith and philosophy in the words and language most accessible for ordinary people. In spite of her best efforts, there is certain vocabulary which can not be avoided in order to convey the actual sense and meaning of the context. The words and concepts are used in their original language and also equivalents in English. The attempt has been made to explain these words in the text and also in the glossary in order to make them clear for readers. References from the *Guru Granth Sahib* are given in Panjabi and their meanings in English in order to support the contents. Many concepts and shared values get frequent repetition which can not be helped due to the nature of the book. The first chapter is on the background to Sikhism covering Sikhs and who they are, the origin of Sikhism, Sikh identity - the five *K*'s, Sikh ethics, the Sikh place of worship – *gurdwara*, Sikh sects and denominations. The second chapter is on the Holy Scripture of Sikhs '*Guru Granth Sahib*'. The third chapter is on the concept of God in Sikhism. It covers the concept and gender of God and the place of *gurus* in Sikhism. The fourth chapter is on the origin of the Universe, ecology and the environment as understood in Sikhism. The fifth chapter is on the equality which covers attitudes of Sikhism on caste, economic and gender inequalities. It also covers Sikh attitudes towards other religions, relationships among people of different religions and nationalities. Chapter six covers family life, marriage, dowry, divorce, family planning and Sikh attitudes on euthanasia or mercy killing. Chapter seven covers Sikh ceremonies and festivals which include life cycle rites of birth, the naming ceremony, marriage and death. It also covers *gurpurabs* and Sikh festivals *Vaisakhi, Diwali, Hola Mohalla, Maghi* and *Lohri*. Chapter eight covers behaviour patterns and includes acceptable behaviour and prohibitions. Chapter nine on 'Roots and Routes' reflects on Sikhism and Christianity. Finally there is a conclusion, glossary and appendices. The appendices included in the book provide information not detailed in the main body of the book but it is necessary to include. The first appendix is on the contributions of the Sikh *gurus* to the Sikh faith and the second appendix is on the glossary. A short bibliography is given at the end so that people interested in this area can advance their knowledge further.

Research Methods

The aim of writing this book is to provide comprehensive information on the basics of Sikhism in a simple and easy to read language. The author has chosen topics which are frequently asked by young adults and also in interfaith meetings. It was also her own curiosity to know Sikhism in depth based on the Holy Scripture. As a mother, she had the experience of her own children's school days and the difficulties faced by them. As a community worker, she heard experiences of other children through their parents. It is unfortunate that this rich, liberal and forward looking religion had little exposure in other languages.

Many Sikhs are now living away from their own home land where Panjabi becomes a second or third language. The whole structure of the *gurdwaras* and religious promotion in diaspora countries is not yet completely geared towards fulfilling the religious and spiritual needs of young Sikhs born and brought up in western countries. The services conducted in the *gurdwaras* are mainly in Panjabi, Sikh authentic literature is mainly in Panjabi and the *katha* and *viakhia* (explanation of Sikh hymns and traditions) are conducted in Panjabi. There is no denying the fact that small efforts are made by most *gurdwaras* such as summer camps, and religious classes in English to meet the growing demand of young Sikhs but still there is a big gap to fill. Many parents even though they are born in Sikh homes and brought up in the Sikh culture and traditions have not always the full capacity to satisfy their children's curiosity logically. The Internet with the different sites on Sikhism is playing a constructive role by responding to many questions asked by those seeking knowledge and to my knowledge many children do use this facility. The main problem found by the author with some of these sites was complicated and difficult vocabulary. A Sikh channel has started recently in the UK. This channel gives some of the programmes and discussions in English which can prove useful for the children born and brought up here. This book is the small contribution made by the author to fill some of the gaps she felt necessary. She tried to explain many concepts and topics to make it easily understood by those who are growing and living in the countries where the Sikh religion and culture are alien to the indigenous culture and media. It is also her passion for the Sikh religion and her concern for the young adults who are not practicing the very basic teachings in their daily life.

The author took a simple approach to research this book. She chose the topics and looked for references from the *Guru Granth Sahib* to find the relevant information. She also consulted other sources on the Holy Book which gave translations of the contents of the *Guru Granth Sahib*. The author checked the interpretations from more than one source to be sure of the accuracy of her explanations. There are certain unresolved topics in Sikhism, for which no unanimous verdicts exist, for example the consumption of meat. Sikhs have a difference of opinion and so far have failed to reach a conclusion. The failure of Sikhs to discriminate between Punjabi culture and Sikh religious tradition is another area which needs looking at. This is one of the reasons that Sikhs could not get rid of caste discrimination in spite of the *gurus'* firm stand on equality and condemnation of caste system. Not many books written on Sikhism were consulted simply because the aim of writing this book was to make it evidence based on the Holy Scripture of Sikhs.

The author was born and brought up in a Sikh family, with a religious environment and strict religious discipline. The family put into practice the Sikh values which were ingrained in her from the very beginning. The girls of the family were given the same privileges and rights as boys. The author had a university education in the 1960's which was rare for girls then. She is fluent in Panjabi and understands both Punjabi and Sikh culture. This family background and her language skills made it easy for her to participate in religious functions and *gurdwara* activities. She has always participated in the *gurdwara* activities and attends the Sikh temple fairly regularly. Her deep understanding of the Sikh way of life, language skills and her experience in being a participant and observer helped her to write this book with understanding.

The author tried to make this book reader friendly by retaining a simple style of writing. She quoted hymns or part of hymns from the *Guru Granth Sahib* in its original language along with the page number in order to introduce the authentic language to the readers. Every effort is made by the author to produce this book purely for educational purposes and not for promotion or propaganda.

Acknowledgement

This book is primarily aimed at young adults both Sikhs and non Sikhs. It also answers the many questions asked in interfaith meetings. I am grateful to Inderjit Singh Bhogal, the Chief Executive of the Yorkshire and Humber Faiths Forum, who encouraged me to undertake this work. He read the first draft of this book carefully and critically. His comments were invaluable for me because of his deep understanding of the Sikh faith and his extensive experience of interfaith work at grassroots as well as strategic level. Since this book is aimed at young adults, Sikhs as well as non Sikhs, it was thought appropriate to seek the views of that age group. Jasdeep Singh Degun, an A-level student studying Religious Education, Music, Sociology and Psychology at Allerton Grange High School, Leeds has very kindly read the first draft of this book and said that schools need this type of material. His comments were extremely useful especially within the context of his experience of reading other books and comparing it with them. They are also useful coming from a student for the level this book has been written. He has a thorough knowledge of Sikhism and has interfaith involvement. I was thrilled when Laura Roberts, the head of RE at Lawnswood High School in Leeds very kindly agreed to read the draft and said that it was excellent. Last but not least my sincere gratitude to Mary White, Administration and Finance Manager at the Yorkshire and Humber Faiths Forum who has diligently checked the final draft of this book out of goodwill and interest of other religions. She found it interesting, readable and informative. She ensured me that it is an easily understood document for those who have little or no knowledge of Sikhism.

I am also grateful for those who let me insert their photographs into the book. It is usual that one gives credit to one's family but in this case it is genuine. My family has been very supportive and understanding especially on the occasions when I felt low and exhausted. My son and daughter invited me for treats and gave me short breaks. I am especially grateful to my son Jas Rait who has willingly offered technical support without which I might be completely lost. I appreciate my husband who let me sit and work for hours.

Satwant Kaur Rait

Chapter 1
Background to Sikhism

1.0 Sikhs and who they are

The word Sikh is believed to be derived from the Panjabi verb `sikhna-ਸਿਖਣਾ`), to learn; the Pali `sikha` (instruction) or the Sanskrit `sisya` meaning learner or disciple. A Sikh is therefore a disciple and a learner, i.e. the one who learns and follows the teachings of ten *gurus* from *Guru* Nanak to *Guru* Gobind Singh (1469-1708) and leads their life according to *gurmat* (guidelines given by *gurus*). It is important for a Sikh to believe only in the teachings of *Sri Guru Granth Sahib* (the Holy Scripture of Sikhs) and not in any other religious doctrine. *Guru Granth Sahib* is the ultimate *Guru* (guide) of the Sikhs and the teachings of *gurus* and contemporary saints are recorded in this Holy Book. The code of conduct called the Sikh *Rahit Maryada* guides the Sikhs in leading their daily life, the performance of religious duties, the importance of the *gurdwara*, reading the Holy Book and living and working in accordance with the principles of *gurmat*.

Sikhism (*Sikhi*) literally means a way of life. It is open to anyone irrespective of ethnicity, colour or creed. It is not for any specific group or community but a message of truth for the whole of humanity. It is important to remember that a Sikh cannot be a Sikh simply by being born into a Sikh family unless he/she adheres to the Sikh teachings. One can not be a Sikh only by believing in the teachings of the Holy Scripture unless he/she behaves and put those teachings in action. There are three distinct terms used for a Sikh and it is important to define them in order to make a clear distinction, i.e. *amritdhari* (initiated or baptised), *kesadhari* (uncut hair and turbaned, headdress religiously obligatory) and *sehajdhari* (clean-shaven). An initiated Sikh is called *amritdhari* who not only keeps the Sikh identity but also attempts to follow the Sikh way of life as well as accepting the doctrines of Sikhism. There are Sikhs who keep an unshorn beard, uncut hair and wear a turban but are not initiated. They are referred to as *kesadhari* Sikhs. There are also *sehajdhari* Sikhs, who believe in the teachings of *Gurus*, but are not initiated and do not maintain an external identity by wearing or using the outward symbols of Sikhism. The word Sikh is used in this book for any person who adheres to the teachings of the Sikh religion and *amritdharis* for initiated Sikhs.

It is believed by some Sikhs that *amritdharis* are the only genuine Sikhs and the other two categories are not true Sikhs. Sikh identity (five 'k's' and code of conduct) given by the tenth *Guru* Gobind Singh by initiating Sikhs and creating *Khalsa Panth* (religious order) is absolutely necessary for complete (sampuran-ਸੰਪੂਰਨ) Sikhs as the *Guru* said "*Rahit pyari mujh ko, Sikh pyara nahin*" (Those adhering to the Sikh teachings and keeping the symbols of faith are dearer than a Sikh to the *Guru*). Many Sikhs interpret '*Rahit*' in a literal term associating only with the five symbols of Sikhism but the actual meaning of '*Rahit*' is much broader and deeper than symbols. The five articles of faith (five 'k's') are a mode of discipline that give a distinct appearance (ਪਹਿਚਾਣ) by which a Sikh can be recognised from among many. The Guru made absolutely clear to Sikhs that adherence to Sikh teachings goes hand-in-hand with external identity which many interpreters tend to ignore. It is important and mandatory to have symbols but most important for a real Sikh is to believe in and lead his/her life according to the principles of the Sikh religion and its ethical values. This internal identity combined with the five symbols draws a complete picture of '*Rahit*'. Any Sikh who, in whatever form, leads a truthful life, does virtuous deeds, loves God's creation, remembers God and submits to God's will is certainly close to God.

2.0 Origin of Sikhism

The Sikh religion was founded by *Guru* Nanak in the fifteenth century in Punjab, a state in northern India. It is the fifth-largest religion in the world and numbers over twenty three million followers. The majority of Sikhs now live in the state of Punjab in India and, prior to the country's partition in 1947, millions of Sikhs lived in what is now known as West Punjab, a province of Pakistan.

Guru Nanak, the founder of the Sikh religion was born in 1469, and decided to crusade against fanaticism and intolerance. He raised his voice against the meaningless rituals and discriminations against the lower castes and women, which were then prevalent in the society. He preached a message of universal love, peace and harmony. He emphasised worship of one God. He taught that the worship of God in whatever religion or tradition one practises it, should be sincere and honest. It became a socio-spiritual phenomenon in Punjab. His religious philosophy and expression has been traditionally known as the *gurmat* (teachings of the *guru*). He was succeeded by nine successor *gurus*. Sikhs believe that the *gurus* were all spiritually one. Over the years, it acquired its own customs, traditions and ceremonies.

Sikhs have distinctive religious values and culture. Their way of life is deeply influenced by Punjabi culture which was cultivated by the values of Hindus, Muslims and Sikhs living together in the undivided Punjab. Cultural and religious values are blended to an extent that on occasions it becomes difficult to distinguish them without an adequate knowledge of Sikhism. There are also denominations in Sikhism presenting views and attitudes which may be different from mainstream Sikhism.

Sikhs are adventurous by nature and do not hesitate to move around for better opportunities. They have settled in many parts of the world such as the Middle East, Africa, Singapore, Malaysia, Australia and many countries of Europe. Sikhs began to settle in western countries at the end of the 19th Century. Britain, the USA and Canada have the highest number of Sikhs outside India. Migration and remigration to various parts of the world especially to countries which have very different sets of values and culture are bound to affect Sikh migrants and their attitude to life. Some Sikhs acquire a new lifestyle suited to themselves with the fusion of eastern and western values. It is important to emphasise the diversity, as well as unifying elements giving continuities to their religious traditions living away from their homeland.

3. 0 Sikh identity - The five *K*'s

Formal initiation into the Sikh faith is traditionally one of the most important and sacred ceremonies of Sikhism and is open to both men and women. It is an expression of full commitment to religion for a Sikh. The initiation ceremony is seen as the way to spiritual development, when coupled with adherence to the ethical principles of Sikhism.

Sikhs were given identity by the tenth *Guru*, Gobind Singh in 1699. He created *Khalsa* (pure ones) and made the initiation ceremony and wearing of the Sikh symbols (the five k's) compulsory which gave them not only a unique and distinctive appearance but also signifies the full commitment of a Sikh to the faith and submission to God. The common identity allows members to form close bonds. Initiated Sikhs wear the five articles of faith, all beginning with the letter '*k*'. The symbols are *kes* (uncut hair), *kangha* (wooden comb), *kirpan* (dagger or sword), *kachha* (cotton knee length undergarment) and *kara* (steel bangle). These symbols have particular significance.

Kes is symbolic of an acceptance of God's will and considered to be a sign of spiritual and moral strength. Sikh men and women are not allowed to cut or remove hair from any part of the body such as head hair, beard and eyebrows. Sikhs wear a turban (*dastar*) to cover their unshorn hair. The Sikh turban is an article of faith which was made mandatory by the founder of the *Khalsa*. It is a symbol of a saint soldier. For Sikhs it is a sign of dedication, self-respect, courage and piety. The turban signifies high moral values. The turban is a symbol of honour and this is the reason that *saropa* (a tradition of giving the turban as an honour) is given to those who have made special contributions towards the community or good causes in *gurdwaras*.

Kangha is a small wooden comb kept by Sikhs in their hair all the time. It is a symbol of personal care and cleanliness, orderly spirituality and discipline of the mind.

Kirpan (sword) is made of two words *kirpa* (compassion) and *an* (honour). It is difficult to find an exact expression in English and the nearest is sword. It is a small or long curved sword worn by initiated Sikhs. It can be  anything from a few inches to three feet long. It is kept in a sheath and can be worn over or under clothing. It is a symbol of freedom from oppression and servility. It signifies dignity and self-respect. Its obvious meaning is of self-defence and individual freedom.

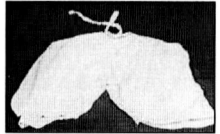

Kachha are specially designed underpants (more like shorts, or drawers) fairly long reaching down to the knees and tight at the bottom. It is a symbol of chastity. This also signifies modesty, moral restraint and continence.

Kara is a steel bangle rather than gold or silver because it is not an ornament, worn on the right wrist. It is a symbol of responsibility and allegiance to God reminding Sikhs that God is eternal with no beginning and no end. It is a symbol that a Sikh is linked to God.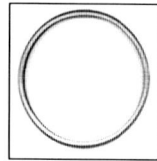

The five articles of faith give a unique appearance and a distinct identity to a Sikh which binds him/her to the *Guru*. For a Sikh it is a sign of allegiance to the Sikh faith.

4.0 Sikh ethics

There are certain ethical principles which are intrinsic to Sikh beliefs and practices. They are also called pillars of ethical living. Foremost amongst these are earning a living with honest and approved means (*kirt karna*), sharing with less fortunate, poor and needy people (*wand chhakna*) and finally reciting the name of God (*naam japna*).

4.1 Kirt karna (earning a living by honest and approved means) puts an emphasis on the strong work ethos. One must work hard for one's living. Money earned through dishonest and deceitful ways has no value in Sikhism. Earning through hypocrisy is also disapproved: ਉਦਰੈ ਕਾਰਣਿ ਆਪਣੇ ਬਹਲੇ ਭੇਖ ਕਰੇਨਿ॥ (GGS 949) which means many adopt deception to appease their hunger. Another example: ਮਖਟੂ ਹੋਇ ਕੈ ਕੰਨ ਪੜਾਏ॥ ਫਕਰੁ ਕਰੇ ਹੋਰੁ ਜਾਤਿ ਗਵਾਏ॥ (GGS: 1245) suggests that a person who is idle and pierces his ears and pretends to be a saint loses his own respect. It is strongly advocated in Sikhism that one should work (work ethics) to earn one's living and not to be a burden on anyone or on the society.

4.2 Wand chhakna (sharing with less fortunate, poor and needy) includes giving money to the needy and sharing food with the poor and hungry. Sikh religious traditions recommend giving *daswandh* (one-tenth of earnings to charitable causes). Sikh families regularly donate money towards *langar* (communal kitchen), the maintenance of *gurdwaras*, charities and other humane causes. It is also suggested that one should use one's commonsense and intelligence in giving help or donations: ਅਕਲੀ ਪਤਿ ਕੈ ਬੁਝੀਐ ਅਕਲੀ ਕੀਚੈ ਦਾਨੁ॥ GGS 1245). It is important for Sikhs to donate whatever they can in case they are not able to give one-tenth of their earnings ਘਾਲਿ ਖਾਇ ਕਿਛੁ ਹਥਹੁ ਦੇਇ॥ ਨਾਨਕ ਰਾਹੁ ਪਛਾਣਹਿ ਸੇਇ॥ (GGS: 1245). Guru Nanak said that earning ethically and sharing with others was the way to God. He also suggested being compassionate and giving to others whatever he/she could: ਦਇਆ ਜਾਣੈ ਜੀਅ ਕੀ ਕਿਛੁ ਪੁੰਨੁ ਦਾਨੁ ਕਰੇਇ॥. Donations and sharing with others should be genuine and free from ego and pride: ਤੀਰਥ ਬਰਤ ਅਰੁ ਦਾਨ ਕਰਿ ਮਨ ਮੈ ਧਰੈ ਗੁਮਾਨੁ॥ ਨਾਨਕ ਨਿਹਫਲ ਜਾਤ ਤਿਹ ਜਿਉ ਕੁੰਚਰ ਇਸਨਾਨੁ॥ (GGS 1428). These two lines explain that pilgrimage, abstinence and giving donations with ego and pride are worthless.

4.3 Naam japna (reciting the name) means that God should always be remembered in the course of everyday life. Sikhs are encouraged to recite *naam*. The aim of life is to be in communion with God and this can be achieved by remembering God's name constantly while working with your hands and feet: ਨਾਮਾ ਕਹੈ ਤਿਲੋਚਨਾ ਮੁਖ ਤੇ ਰਾਮੁ ਸੰਮਾਲਿ॥ ਹਾਥ ਪਾਉ ਕਰਿ ਕਾਮੁ ਸਭੁ ਚੀਤੁ ਨਿਰੰਜਨ ਨਾਲਿ॥ (GGS:1376). *Naam japna* (recitation) is not mere repetition of words. It performs three functions i.e. removing evils; giving the knowledge of truth, goodness and beauty and bringing out a merger of the individual into the supreme. The true remembrance of the *naam* is a three fold activity i.e. meditation with words, mind and actions; humility and good thinking and performance of noble deeds. This is one of the reasons that truthful living is considered higher than truth in Sikhism. Reciting the name of God is meaningless unless the mind is pure: ਕਾਹੇ ਕਉ ਕੀਜੈ ਧਿਆਨੁ ਜਪੰਨਾ॥ ਜਬ ਤੇ ਸੁਧੁ ਨਾਹੀ ਮਨੁ ਅਪਨਾ॥ (GGS 485). This hymn was uttered by saint Namdeo which asks how one can think of reciting the name of God when one's mind is impure. There is also a similar message conveyed by the third guru: ਮਨਿ ਮੈਲੈ ਭਗਤਿ ਨ ਹੋਵਈ ਨਾਮੁ ਨ ਪਾਇਆ ਜਾਇ)(GGS: 39) that a polluted mind devotes not to the "Word" and receives not God's name.

Sikhism teaches that those who practice and lead their life according to these ethical values will automatically accept the will of God. This means believing that everything happens according to the will of God or under God's order (*hukam*-ਹੁਕਮ) and it should be accepted (*bhana manana*-ਭਾਣਾ ਮੰਨਣਾ-accepting the will of God) without mourning or complaining. One should remain the same in happiness and in grief.

5.0 Core values

Those mentioned above are the three main pillars in Sikhism. Sikhism stresses other core values, which are important for any Sikh and Sikhs are obliged to understand and practice them in their life. These core values support ethical principles and are interdependent. For example, voluntary service supports sharing with the needy and poor and the two can not be performed without belief in equality. The relationship between ethical codes and core values is clear.

5.1 Seva (voluntary service) is highly valued and essential in the Sikh religion. The Sikh *gurus* made seva (voluntary service) a prerequisite to spiritual development. The ideal of a true Sikh is to look beyond the self and to serve one's fellow beings. *Seva* is a service to the community at large or helping to meet a particular need for the benefit of others. It should be selfless. There are three types of voluntary service i.e. physical, economic and mental. Voluntary service in physical form means doing service with your hands such as cleaning and sweeping the *gurdwara*, cooking in the community kitchen, looking after the weak, disabled and old. Economic service means donating money towards charitable and humane causes. *Daswandh* (one-tenth of one's income) is recommended in Sikhism to fulfill this obligation. Mental service is enlightening others by encouraging them to gain knowledge and making them aware of the reality and true facts.

5.2 Equality is a key concept in the Sikh religion. It implies gender and social equality. The Sikh concept of equality applies to both men and women in secular and religious life. Sikhism advocates gender equality and accords women an equal status in society. They should not be treated as subservient to men and mere perpetuators of the race. They play a dominant role in preparing the future generations. They are the first teachers of their children and bind them socially. Therefore they should be respected and valued. Social equality covers caste, status, colour and creed. The teachings of Sikhism categorically reject using the caste system as a pretext for promoting inequality. The Sikh religion also promotes a classless society, giving more importance to virtue than wealth. The status of an individual should be determined by deeds or merits and not by class position and status. All human beings are children of God and a person should be judged by his/her actions and not on the basis of caste, status, colour and creed.

5.3 Other beliefs associated with Sikhism form the base of Sikh philosophy. The Sikh *gurus* regarded the world as real and meaningful. Sikhism advocates full participation in life and it establishes the primacy of family life. In fact normal family life is the medium of spiritual training and expression. Renunciation is not favoured in Sikhism. Sikhism accepts the theory of *karma* (taking responsibility for one's actions) and transmigration of souls from one life to another. The idea of *mukti* (transmigration of the soul until its ultimate union with God) was given a new concept of striving for a moral and spiritual mode of living. Sikh *gurus* repeatedly emphasised that *haumen* (individualism or self-centredness) is at the root of the problems from which the individual and society suffer. One should free oneself from the evil manifestations of *haumen*, i.e. lust, anger, greed, attachment and pride and replace them with five virtuous qualities self-control, forgiveness, contentment, love for God and humility. Sikhs are advised to abstain from *halal* (meat slaughtered by the process of slow and ritual killing), intoxicants, adultery and polygamy.

6.0 Sikh place of worship - Gurdwara

Faith is sustained through places of worship. The place of Sikh worship is called a *gurdwara* which literally means 'the doorway to God'. It is also called a *gurughar* meaning 'house of the Lord' and Sikh temple (Sikh place of worship). It is easily visible from a distance because of the Sikh flag *Nishan Sahib*, which is flown quite high outside all the

gurdwaras. It is the ensign of the *Khalsa Panth*, an expression of authority and commands a high level of respect. It is triangular in shape and saffron in colour and has a symbol of *Khanda* ☬ which constitutes three symbols in one. This is a double edged straight sword with concave edges placed in the middle of the symbol which represents the oneness of God and also means to cut evils both ways. It is surrounded by a circle with two curved swords. The two curved swords flanking the circle represent temporal (*meeri*) and spiritual (*peeri*) authority of the Sikh gurus. The circle denotes no beginning and no end signifying the continuation of life. *Nishan Sahib* is normally changed on every *Vaisakhi* which celebrates the birthday of the *Khalsa*.

It is an essential institution for Sikhs because of the congregational nature of the religion and the importance given to the *sangat* (congregation) by the Sikh *gurus*. Sikh *gurus* gave the *sangat* a status higher than that of a *guru*. The *gurus* made it clear that attendance at communal worship is a necessary part of the spiritual life of a Sikh.

The *gurdwara* is central to the lives of Sikhs as all the lifecycle rites such as birth, initiation, naming and wedding ceremonies take place there. The last journey of death also departs finally from a *gurdwara*. There are a number of other functions and festivals taking place all around the year such as *gurpurabs* (anniversaries and special events in the lives of the *gurus*), *sangrand*, the first day of the lunar month and some other festivals such as *Vaisakhi, Diwali, Hola Mohalla, Maghi* and *Lohri*. *Gurdwaras* promote the Sikh religion and Sikh traditions. The essential characteristic of a *gurdwara* is that a copy of the *Guru Granth Sahib* is always kept in the main hall which is opened, read and closed every day with great respect. It is kept under a canopy and the *chauri* (which consists of a yak tail hair or artificial fibre set in a wooden or metal holder) is waved over the sacred 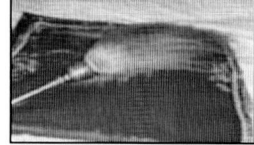 book as a sign of respect. This is the highest spiritual authority for Sikhs and they are instructed to follow the *shabad* (word-bani) and teachings of the Sikh Scripture. Sikhs treat their Holy Book as a living *Guru*. Guru Gobind Singh proclaimed that after him, there would be no more human *gurus* for the Sikhs, and they would follow *Guru Granth Sahib*-the '*Word Guru*' (ਬਾਣੀ ਗੁਰੂ ਗੁਰੂ ਹੈ ਬਾਣੀ: GGS: 982). He installed the *Granth Sahib* as an ultimate and permanent *Guru* of Sikhs. Both men and women can read the *Guru Granth Sahib* and can officiate at Sikh ceremonies if they have competency in *Gurmukhi*. The *gurdwara* is open to the public every day and can be visited by any person irrespective of religion, sex and colour. A *granthi* or *bhai* (priest) acts as caretaker, and is also skilled in reciting *gurbani* and doing *kirtan* (hymn singing). *Granth Sahib* is written in *ragas* (musical mode) and the hymns from this Holy Book are sung in *kirtan*. *Kirtan* (hymn-singing) and *viakhia* (explaining the original text in simple Panjabi) often forms part of daily and weekly prayers.

Sikhs attend the *gurdwara* as a family. Before entering the prayer hall, as a mark of respect, shoes must be removed and the head must be covered. On entering the hall, Sikh worshippers kneel, touching the floor with their foreheads before the *Guru Granth Sahib*. Worshippers usually make a voluntary offering of money in front of *Guru Granth Sahib*. Some also take flowers, sugar, milk and fruit with them as offerings. All people sit on the floor of the prayer hall, women on one side and men on the other side in order to avoid physical contact and distraction from the opposite sex. It is also a part of the Punjabi cultural tradition.

Gurdwaras provide exceptional facilities. *Langar* (communal food) is served in almost all *gurdwaras* as part of Sikh religious traditions and also accommodation is offered to those visiting a *gurdwara*, free of any charge. Most *gurdwaras* offer religion, music and Panjabi language teaching and maintain a library for its members. Provisions are also made for social activities such as youth clubs, women's groups, welfare provision and elderly day centres making *gurdwaras* a source of networking and information for Sikhs. A *gurdwara* is therefore, a multipurpose institution for Sikhs. It binds them together religiously and socially and becomes a unifying force in a crisis. Donation from the *sangat* is the main source of the *gurdwara* income. The Sikh *sangat* generally donates generously at weekly *diwans* and on special occasions. The *gurdwaras* depend on voluntary *seva* (service) and Sikh *sevadars* (volunteers) offer their services with dedication to run and manage *gurdwaras*. Historical *gurdwaras* in Punjab are managed by the *Shiromani Gurdwara Prabandhak Committee* (SGPC) based in Amritsar (Punjab). The SGPC does not only manage the security, finance, facility maintenance and religious aspects of *gurdwaras* but is also a decisive body on religious matters. The Sikh Code of Conduct (*Rahit Maryada*) was released by this body. *Gurdwaras* in the United Kingdom are managed by committees elected democratically by the Sikh *sangat*. The executive committee is formed from within this committee, which takes the responsible positions of management. The committees are fully accountable to the *sangat* for their decisions and actions while in office through general and extraordinary meetings.

7.0 Sikh denominations and saint preachers

Sikhism is a relatively recent religion but like any other religion it has denominations and manifestations. After the death of *Guru* Gobind Singh in 1708, there were a number of factors which influenced the practices of Sikh religious traditions. Sikh sovereignty under *Maharaja* Ranjit Singh brought peace and prosperity for Sikhs for nearly half a century. However, Sikh religious practices faded under the management of his non-Sikh officers, while the annexation of the Punjab by the British in 1849, and subsequent events witnessed the further lapse of Sikh values. The Sikh religion grew amidst the two most powerful and influential religions and had to constantly safeguard its distinctiveness. This gave birth to reform and spiritual movements which could keep the Sikh religion and religious traditions intact. From time to time different denominations and manifestations appeared. Many saint preachers spread the message of gurus. It is not within the scope of this book to mention all but just a few which still exist and are influential.

7.1 Namdharis: This is a Sikh reform movement which originated in the nineteenth century. It began with *Baba* Balak Singh (1785-1862) and developed under the leadership of his successor *Baba* Ram Singh. Namdharis contributed enormously to the revival of Sikhism and the Indian freedom struggle. The headquarters of the *Namdhari* movement are based at *Bhaini Sahib* in Ludhiana (Punjab), the birth place of *Baba* Ram Singh.

Literally, *Namdhari* means one who upholds the name of God and its name originated from the importance placed by *Baba* Ram Singh upon the practice of *naam-japna* (recital or meditation on the name of God). In India, they are also known as *Kukas*, from the Panjabi noun *Kuk*, this is related to their practice of reciting the gurbani in a high pitched style. They wear white clothing and are easily identified by the way they tie their turban horizontally across the forehead. According to *Namdhari* tradition, the tenth *guru*, Gobind Singh did not die at Nander in 1708, but continued his mission under the name of Ajapal Singh until 1812. They also believe that *Guru* Gobind Singh did not confer the *Guru-ship* upon the *Adi Granth* but installed Balak Singh as his successor. *Namdhari* Sikhs believe in the living *guru*. They pay great respect to *Guru Granth Sahib* although they do not believe it to be their *guru*. They make a distinction between the guru and the *Granth Sahib*. Their *guru* takes precedence over the *Granth Sahib*. Their present *guru* is Jagatjit Singh nominated in 1959 thus demonstrating their belief in the continuity of and succession of *gurus*.

Namdharis strictly adhere to the teachings of Sikh *gurus* and protested against moral laxity within the Sikh *Panth* especially the use of drugs, alcohol, meat eating, ostentatious wedding ceremonies and dowries. They stressed simple wedding ceremonies (though their weddings are performed differently from a Sikh wedding 'Anand karaj' as bride and groom walk around the *havan*-holy fire). They condemned infanticide. They were against caste system among Sikhs and advocated inter-caste marriages and remarriage of widows. They strongly believed in *daswandh*, which means donating one-tenth of their earnings to religious and humane causes. All *Namdharis* are initiated Sikhs and their initiation ceremony is called *naam-laina* (receiving the *guru's* word, or *gurmantar*). The *gurmantar* is given by their spiritual *guru* and it is the secret bond between the guru and his disciple, which must never be divulged. They do not distribute *karah prasad* though a *prasad* of dried fruit is usually distributed at the end of *Namdhari diwans*.

Namdhari Sikhs are strict vegetarians. They eat food cooked by *Sodhis* (one who follows the code of the discipline of *Namdharis* only). They are prohibited from consuming meat or liquor, smoking tobacco and having extra marital relationships. Some of their beliefs distinguish them from other mainstream Sikhs in spite of their firm commitment to most Sikh teachings.

7.2 Nirankaris: *Nirankari* literally means one who believes in the formless God. It was a spiritual regeneration movement placing the emphasis upon spirituality rather than what they regard as the militant ideal of the *Khalsa*. *Baba* Dyal (1783-1855) founded it during the period of Sikh rule in the Punjab. He observed the gradual emergence of ritualistic practices in Sikhs and made an attempt to revive the Sikh way of worship, life and conduct. He strongly rejected idolatry and ritualistic practices. He preached bowing only before *Guru Granth Sahib* and worshipping *Nirankar* (the formless God). He also preached against consumption of intoxicants and meat. Historically his most significant and noble reform was the introduction of *Anand karaj*, the simple Sikh marriage ceremony in the presence of the *Guru Granth Sahib* and the recital of *lavan* (wedding hymns from the *Granth Sahib*). He contributed towards the simplification of Sikh rites of passage. The character of Sikh ceremonies today owes much to this movement. Marriage and other ceremonies are fixed without consulting astrologers and there are no payments made for the performance of ceremonies. No dowry is displayed at weddings. They reject the caste system and preach the harmony and respect for all human beings. They believe in the teachings of the Sikh gurus but do not regard the *Granth Sahib* as their *guru*. *Nirankaris* believe in the necessity of a human *guru*. There is no particular initiation ceremony, but the *Nirankaris* whisper their secret naam (word) in the ear of new followers thus making them different from other mainstream Sikhs.

Their *diwan* is called *sangat*. They sing shabads (hymns) from the *Granth Sahib* and *Avtar Bani* (compositions of *guru* Avtar Singh). They do not recite ardas (concluding prayer) or distribute prasad at the end of their *diwan*. Usually they prepare *langar* (communal food) for the congregation, which is served to men and women in the same hall.

Nirankaris have their headquarters in Delhi where their guru lives and it has become their place of pilgrimage. The *Nirankaris* publish literature in many languages for distribution to the public.

7.3 Radhasoamis: The term '*Radhasoami*' literally means union of the soul with God. It is made up of two words: *Radha* (wife or soul) and *Soami* (husband or Lord) means the 'Lord of the soul'. Their main emphasis is on the attainment of spiritual unity with God through *naamsimran* (meditation on God's name) and *satsang* (congregation of truthful people). They do not believe in any religious rituals.

This movement was established by Shiv Dayal Singh (1818-1878) in 1861 and named *Radhasoami Satsang*. According to *Radhasoami* beliefs, the *satguru* (true teacher) is the giver of light. They believe in a living guru (teacher), who will teach human beings the meaning of *naam* (God's word) in order to attain spiritual unity with God. However, for this purpose, an individual must listen to the *shabad* (word) or *naam* (name) of the Lord. *Radhasoamis* also preach the importance of vegetarianism for achieving salvation. It is important for them to keep high levels of morality; they practice *shabad* yoga meditation, and abstinence from alcohol and drugs.

Radhasoamis sit on chairs in their *satsang* and do not remove their shoes. They do not display any religious books on a platform or any pictures in the congregation hall. Their *diwan* (religious meeting) culminates in a sermon, which is based on the *sant* (saint) tradition of Northern India. *Prasad* is reserved for special occasions, such as the anniversary of the birth of their gurus. *Radhasoamis* use nuts in their *prasad* and it is served on plates and eaten with utensils rather than by hand. The use of nuts and sultanas in *karah prasad* is strictly forbidden in the Sikh religion. The tradition of *langar* (free kitchen) is also different in the *Radhasoami* practice. *Langar* is prepared every day at their headquarters in *Beas* in India. It is given free to the poor, but other people buy it at a reduced rate.

Their *guru* lives in *Beas*, which is a *dera* (headquarters) of *Radhasoamis* and has become the place of pilgrimage for them. The *guru* nominates his successor when he feels that his end is near. The person chosen is usually his closest disciple. The national secretary of the *Radhasoami satsang* is appointed by their *satguru*. Local secretaries are responsible for looking after the affairs of local *satsangs* and their appointments are also made by *satguru*.

The reform movements saved the Sikh religion from decline and made timely contributions. The principle of a continuous succession and presence of a supreme spiritual authority forever in a living *guru* distinguished them from mainstream Sikhism.

7.4 Saint preachers

There are many well known saints who tried to spread the message of Sikh gurus and brought many within the Sikh fold. Their deep commitment to Sikhism influenced others to follow them. It is not possible to mention all but as an example two are mentioned who are much more popular in the west.

7.4.1 The 3H organisation: The 3H stands for healthy, happy and holy. This organisation, also known as Sikh *Dharma* Brotherhood, was founded by Harbhajan Singh Puri popularly known as Bhajan *Yogi* or *Yogi* Bhajan in 1971 in North America. It was an interesting development within the Sikh movement in North America where it attracted a number of white American followers. They are baptised Sikhs and strictly follow the Sikh code of conduct. Both men and women wear turbans and usually dress in white. They learn *shabad kirtan* even though they do not always read Panjabi. They are very dedicated to the Sikh traditions and follow them immaculately. I have seen them performing their daily routine which includes yoga, meditation, *naam simran* and *shabad kirtan*.

7.4.2 *Guru* Nanak *Nishkam Sevak Jatha*: The leader of this *Jatha* (organisation) was *Baba* Puran Singh *Kerichowala* (Kericho is the name of an East African town), who migrated to East Africa in the 1930s where he began preaching the message of the Sikh *gurus*. Sikh values had lapsed among East African Sikhs. He gathered many followers in East Africa. He came to Britain in the early 1970's and attracted a large number of followers in the Midlands, where they set up their first *gurdwara* in Birmingham, known as *Guru Nanak Nishkam Jatha*. *Babaji* died in June 1983. This began as a regional organisation in East Africa to revive Sikhism among East African Sikhs and is now spreading in other parts of the world.

Followers of *Baba* Puran Singh observe the Sikh code of conduct very strictly. They are initiated Sikhs. Baba Puran Singh's main emphasis was on *amrit chhako te singh sajo te naam japo* (take *amrit* and be proper Sikhs by keeping *rahit* - Sikh symbols, and meditate on the name of God). They do not allow women and non-*amritdhari* (not initiated) Sikhs to participate in the reading of the *Granth Sahib* at *Akhand path* (continuous reading) and *sadharan path* (ordinary religious reading) ceremonies. They are pure vegetarians and abstain from alcohol and any other intoxicants. The *gurdwaras* managed by *Jatha* do not have elected committees. The living *Babaji* (leader of the organisation) appoints *jathedars* (leader of the *Jatha*) to manage *gurdwaras*. Though they are not democratically elected yet they are accountable for their actions to *Babaji*. This accountability helps to run these *gurdwaras* smoothly and effectively.

Saint preachers spread the message of Sikh *gurus* and made a valuable contribution towards Sikhism though in many cases unique traditions are established known as *sant maryada*. Sikhs should strictly follow one *maryada* and that is a *gur maryada* (teachings of *Guru Granth Sahib*) and should bow only in front of *Guru Granth Sahib* and no one else.

8.0 Summary

A Sikh is a disciple of ten *gurus* and believes and practices the teachings of *Guru Granth Sahib*. Sikhism is a way of life which can be followed by anyone irrespective of their caste, class, colour and creed. It is a religion for the whole of humanity and not that of any specific group or community. It is regarded as a distinct faith bringing radical changes to the existing society suffering from inequality and fanaticism. It promotes gender and social equality and recommends voluntary service to the wider community. Sikhs believe in one God. The Sikh tenets include the requirement to earn a living with honest and approved means, share with poor and needy, remember the name of God and submit to God's will. It however, rejects renunciation or austerities and the caste system. It also denounces superstitions and meaningless rituals. It emphasises the leading of a family life unattached to gross materialism. Sikhs are easily recognised by their distinct appearance, an identity given by the tenth *guru*, Gobind Singh through the initiation ceremony. This is known as the five '*k*'s, all beginning with '*k*' i.e. *kes, kangha, kachh, kara* and *kirpan*. The Sikh religion is a congregational religion, and therefore a place of worship is important for Sikhs. A Sikh place of worship is called *gurdwara* which is a multipurpose centre. Sikhs celebrate lifecycle rites, *gurpurabs* (the anniversaries and other important events of their *gurus*), *sangrand,* the first day of the lunar month and other festivals such as *Vaisakhi, Diwali, Hola Mohalla, Lohri* and *Maghi* in the *gurdwaras*. There are denominations and manifestations in Sikhism which originated from time to time aiming to revive Sikhism and saving it from decline. Almost all denominations believed in the living spiritual *guru* making them distinct from mainstream Sikhism. Many saint preachers though spread the message of *Gurus* created their own traditions known as *sant maryada*. Sikhs should own only *Gur-maryada* (teachings of *Guru Granth Sahib*).

Chapter 2
The Holy Scripture of the Sikhs

1.0 Guru Granth Sahib

The *Guru Granth Sahib* is the holy scripture of the Sikhs, originally known as *Adi Granth* interpreted as original or eternal scripture. Although the word '*Adi*' means first, it is not used to mean first in a sequential sense. It means "original" within this context. "The *Adi Granth* is a way of expressing the belief that Sikhism did not begin with the ministry of *Guru* Nanak but has its origin in eternity" (Cole and Sambhi. 1990: 32).

It was compiled by the fifth Sikh *guru*, Arjan Dev. He collected the compositions of his four predecessors and also added his own hymns along with some of the popular sayings of Hindu devotees and Muslim saints and mystics. *Bhai* Gurdas, one of the devout Sikhs scribed this Granth under the supervision and guidance of *Guru* Arjan Dev. This work was started in 1601 and was finished in 1604. In 1604, this *Granth* was installed at *Harmandar Sahib*, the house or temple of God, now known as the Golden Temple situated in Amritsar. It is a central place for the Sikh faith and was also built by the fifth *guru* Arjan Dev in 1598. By this time Sikhs had their own temple and Holy Scripture indicating the process of emergence and maturity of Sikh traditions.

The second and final version of this *Granth* was dictated by the tenth *guru* Gobind Singh to *Bhai* Mani Singh. He added the hymns of his father, *Guru* Tegh Bahadur (ninth *guru*) and possibly one couplet of his own and finalised it in 1705 at Damdama *Sahib* in the village of Talwandi Sabo, Bathinda in Punjab. *Guru* Gobind Singh terminated the line of human *gurus* by bestowing *guruship* on the *Adi Granth*. He conferred the title of Guru on 6th October 1708 before his death after which it was called *Guru Granth Sahib*. It is acknowledged as an authorised version. *Guru Granth Sahib* is the only world scripture which was collected and put together during the life time of its compilers and for Sikhs it is their ultimate *Guru*.

The *Guru Granth Sahib* contains the compositions of the first five Sikh *gurus* with the addition of *Guru* Tegh Bahadur and possibly one couplet of *Guru* Gobind Singh. It also includes the poetry and songs written or uttered by Hindu and

Muslim Saints and mystics who expressed the common concepts such as absurdity of religious rituals, the hatred of idolatry, castelessness and gender equality between the 12th Century and 17th Century in different parts of India. The compositions and utterances of the high and low born are included irrespective of their caste and status. Obviously, the idea of *Guru* Arjan Dev was to affirm the fundamental unity of all religions, and the unitary character of all mystic experience. This was done at a time when the caste system was deep rooted in Indian society. It was the uniqueness of this *Granth* to have such insertions at the time when society was suffering from inequality, factionalism and fanaticism. The style in which the *Granth* is written appears transparent, open and uncompromising with the inclusion of satires on tyrannical rulers, fanatical clergies and sects and fake hermits. Hardly any other scripture of that stature is completely free from bias, hostility and controversy. It also illustrates the social, economic and religious condition of India during this period.

The *Granth* is written in a language spoken and understood by lay people. It is clear that the *Granth* is written in Panjabi using *Gurmukhi* script popularised by *Guru* Angad, the second guru though there is a difference of opinion about the origin and antiquity of the Panjabi language. However, it is generally accepted that the language of the *Adi Granth* is Panjabi. The language principally employed is the language of the saints (*Sant bhasha*) generally known as Hindvi, a mixture of Hindi, Prakrit, Brij and Panjabi evolved during the medieval period. It also has expressions from Sanskrit, Persian and Arabic. The collection of hymns added to the *Adi Granth* composed by saints of different regions has allowed for variations and local dialects. So, not only in subject matters, or religious affiliations of its authors, but also in language, the Granth upholds the synthesis of creeds as against exclusiveness of form. The poetic style is very appealing because of its powerful expressions, directness and resilience. The main purpose of *gurus* was to get their message across to the ordinary people in a way which was appealing to their ears, minds and hearts.

The entire *bani* (hymns) printed in its current format comes to 1430 pages and is divided into 33 sections. The *Granth* contains 5894 hymns in all, out of which the largest number of compositions are by *Guru* Arjan (2216), *Guru* Nanak (976), *Guru* Angad (61), Amar Das (907), Ram Das (679), Tegh Bahadur (118), and *bhaktas* and bards (937) (Gopal Singh. 1984: XIX). Most of it is written in classical *ragas* (musical scores). Music forms the basis of the classification of the hymns. The hymns are further classified according to the musical clef or key (*ghar*) in which each is to be sung. The *Granth* is arranged firstly according to the *raga*, secondly, according to the nature or metre of the hymn, thirdly authorship, and fourthly the key. The integral relationship between music and verse has been maintained throughout with scholarly rectitude and concern. Furthermore, each psalm or hymn is preceded by a number (*mohalla*) which denotes the name of the composer *guru* from *Guru* Nanak onwards. It may be noted that the "apostolic" succession extends from the first to the tenth *guru*, and that the *gurus* are often referred to reverentially by their place in the order. What is more, each *guru* speaks in the name of the founder *guru* whose spirit permeates his successors.

The Sikh philosophy as embodied in the *Guru Granth Sahib* is chiefly a philosophy of action, deed and consequence. It explains the genesis of the world and the ultimate nature of reality. It is a science of reality and the art of union with reality. It gives a vision of truth, and it opens up new paths for the mind of man (Mansukhani: 249). The emphasis is on a shared communal experience, purpose of life, active involvement and controlling the five evils. An ideal Sikh should be able to cultivate the qualities of contemplation on the *naam* while engaging him/her self in worldly affairs. It offers a perfect set of values and a practical code of conduct. It includes numerous hymns on the glory of God and the path to spiritual salvation. The main doctrine of the *Granth Sahib* is related to the nature and attributes of God and the means by which salvation may be attained. The *Granth* does not ignore the spiritual and creative side of man. It symbolises that all should treat one another as brothers and sisters (universal harmony- ਸਾਂਝੀ ਵਾਲਤਾ) and focus on the welfare of whole humanity (ਸਰਬਤ ਦਾ ਭਲਾ). The *Granth Sahib* has given great importance to the 'word' (ਸ਼ਬਦ). The 'word' of the *Guru* is the music which the seers hear in their moments of ecstasy: the 'word' of the *Guru* is the highest scripture. By communion with the 'word', one attains the vision unattainable. It also promotes the message of gurus that the truthful living is higher than truth is. For Sikhs, "Word is *Guru* and *Guru* is the Word - ਬਾਣੀ ਗੁਰੂ ਗੁਰੂ ਹੈ ਬਾਣੀ" (GGS: 982).

The concept of *naam* forms the central thesis of the Sikh philosophy of religion. The name of God is said to be the only refuge for a man in this worldly existence.

"Ek ot eko adharu ਏਕ ਓਟ ਏਕੋ ਆਧਾਰੁ
Nanak magai namu prabh saru ਨਾਨਕੁ ਮਾਗੈ ਨਾਮੁ ਪ੍ਰਭ ਸਾਰੁ॥
(Thou, O Lord Art my only shelter, my only support
Nanak asks for thy excellent name, my master)" GGS: 289

It is also said to be the most valuable possession of worldly man.
"Bin navai sabh koi niradhan satgur bujh bujhai
ਬਿਨੁ ਨਾਵੈ ਸਭੁ ਕੋਈ ਨਿਰਧਨੁ ਸਤਿਗੁਰਿ ਬੂਝ ਬੁਝਾਈ॥੪॥
(*Satguru* has given me understanding
Without the Name, everyone is impoverished)" GGS: 1232

It is called nectar (*amrit*) and is obtained rarely.

"Vah vah amrit naam hai ਵਾਹੁ ਵਾਹੁ ਅੰਮ੍ਰਿਤ ਨਾਮੁ ਹੈ
Gurmukh pavai koi ਗੁਰਮੁਖਿ ਪਾਵੈ ਕੋਇਆ
(Blessed! Blessed is the Nectar Name
Which a few holy men obtain)" GGS: 515

Guru Granth Sahib is a living *Guru* for the Sikhs which guides and advises them. It deserves the status of a living *guru* rather than just a religious book. This is the reason that it is always kept on a raised platform under a canopy covered in expensive cloth called *romalla*, whether it is at the *gurdwara* or at home. A *chauri* (whisk) is waved over it when it is read. The canopy and a whisk are symbols of authority. As a sign of respect and reverence for the Holy Scripture, Sikhs take off their shoes, and cover their head before bowing and taking a seat in front of *Guru Granth Sahib*. Every *gurdwara* must display this Holy Book which should be opened, read and closed every day. It is used by the Sikhs for all occasions and ceremonies at the time of birth, marriage and death.

2.0 Summary

The Holy Scripture of Sikhs is called *Guru Granth Sahib* originally known as *Adi Granth* meaning original or eternal book. The *Granth Sahib* is considered to be the living embodiment of *Gurus* and the ultimate *Guru* of Sikhs. It was first compiled in 1604 by the fifth guru Arjan Dev who collected the compositions of his predecessors and added his own to it. Apart from the compositions of the *gurus*, it contains the teachings of saints and mystics belonging to different classes, castes and religions from different regions of India covering the period from the 12th to 17th Century. *Bhai* Gurdas scribed this *Granth* under the supervision and guidance of *Guru* Arjan Dev. This was installed in *Harmandar Sahib* now known as the Golden Temple at Amritsar. Gobind Singh, the tenth and last Sikh *guru*, added to the *Adi Granth*, hymns of his father, *Guru* Tegh Bahadur, and possibly one couplet of his own in 1705. He bestowed it with the *Guruship* in 1708, putting an end to the tradition of *guruship* in an individual person. He ordered the cessation of the line of a living *guru* and installed the *Granth* as an ultimate and permanent *Guru* of Sikhs. Since then, it was named as *Guru Granth Sahib*. This is the only scripture of the world which was collected and put together during the life time of its compilers and whose authenticity has never been questioned. It is written in poetry form using *ragas* and both music and poetry have formed an inseparable part of the Sikh rituals and the Sikh cultural pattern. *Gurus* employed homely and simple metaphors. It was written in Panjabi using the *Gurmukhi* script. By far the largest portion of the *Granth* was composed in Hindvi, a mixture of western Hindi, Prakrit, Brij and Panjabi. There is also the use of Sanskrit, Arabic and Persian words. So, not only in subject matters, or religious affiliations of its authors, but also in language, the *Granth* upholds the synthesis of creeds as against exclusiveness of form. It is also a socio-cultural history of the medieval period particularly of North India. It gives the message of love, harmony, equality and human dignity, service towards humanity, caring for God's creation, remembering God and doing good deeds in order to liberate the soul aiming for an ultimate unity with God. It includes numerous hymns on the glory of God and the path to spiritual salvation. The *Granth* does not ignore the spiritual and creative side of man. This *Granth* is not only meant for Sikhs but also for all people who believe in the existence of God and love for humanity and God's creation.

Chapter 3

The Concept of God in Sikhism

1.0 The concept of God in Sikhism

The pattern of the universe and the regularity of the laws behind its working have brought many to believe that there is a power controlling the universe. Some call it nature and others supreme power, God or Lord of the universe. There is no scientific evidence to prove or disprove the existence of God. It is the experience and testimony of saints and realisation of great spiritual souls that mentions the existence of God. Sikhism believes in the existence of God, a supreme power. *Guru* Nanak's perception and understanding of the nature of God is clearly given in his composition known as the *Mool Mantra*, a fundamental creed that literally means the 'Root Formula'. This fundamental creed of the Sikh people is written at the very beginning of *Granth Sahib* reflecting the Sikh's belief in monotheism (one God). The original text along with translation states:

"*Ek O ankar* (There is One and only One God)
Satnam (It is an Eternal Truth or true is God's name)
Karta Purakh (Creator)
Nirbhau (without fear)
Nirvair (without enmity)
Akal Murat (Timeless and formless)
Ajuni (beyond the cycle of birth and death) *Saibhan* (self-existent)
Gurprasad (Realised by Divine Grace)
Adi sach (true in the beginning)
jugad sach (true in the primeval age)
hai bhi sach (true God is), *Nanak hosi bhi sach* (Nanak says true God shall be)
ੴ ਸਤਿਨਾਮੁ ਕਰਤਾ ਪੁਰਖੁ ਨਿਰਭਉ ਨਿਰਵੈਰੁ ਅਕਾਲ ਮੂਰਤਿ ਅਜੂਨੀ ਸੈਭੰ ਗੁਰਪ੍ਰਸਾਦਿ ॥
ਆਦਿ ਸਚੁ ਜੁਗਾਦਿ ਸਚੁ ॥ ਹੈ ਭੀ ਸਚੁ ਨਾਨਕ ਹੋਸੀ ਭੀ ਸਚੁ ॥ " (GGS:1)

The *Mool Mantra* is constituted of two components - *Ek* and *Oankar* (ੴ). *Ek* means one, and is written as a numerical figure '੧' before *Oankar*, thus enhancing his firm conviction in the oneness of God. Its main importance and underlying significance lies in the fact that one is not represented by words, but by a numerical figure '੧'; thus completely eliminating any possibility of under valuing it's interpretation. His was 'One and Only One' Supreme Being, an indivisible entity. *Oankar* stands for God thus emphasising the notion of the oneness of God. The frequent occurrence of this in the Sikh Scripture *Guru Granth Sahib* signifies the centrality of this belief.

Many Sikhs meditate upon naam and use *Ek-Oankar* for '*Naam Simran*' (reciting the name of God) as this is considered to be a most powerful *Mantra* for achieving spiritual progress and Divine Grace for final emancipation of the individual soul. In conclusion, it can be said that *Ek-Oankar* (ੴ) is the main symbol of Sikhism given by *Guru* Nanak based on his spiritual experience and inspired vision at the very inception of the Sikh faith.

The Sikh belief in monotheism contradicts the doctrine of incarnation (God born in human form). As God is infinite, eternal and beyond the cycle of life and death, so God can not incarnate God's own self into what is known as *avtara* (God in human form). Therefore, in relation to God the doctrine of reincarnation (ਅਵਤਾਰ) makes no sense in Sikhism. Since God is without any form, colour and lineage, God can not be installed as an idol. Sikhism is strongly against idol worship.

God is both transcendent (*nirgun*-abstract) and immanent (*sargun*-fully present). The nature of God in transcendent condition is abstract (*nirgun* without any attributes) being formless, boundless and beyond human knowledge. God becomes immanent when manifested in God's own creation. God becomes pervasive therefore immanent. *Guru* Amar Das says, "This world that you see is the manifestation of the Lord. It is the Lord that you see ਏਹੁ ਵਿਸੁ ਸੰਸਾਰੁ ਤੁਮ ਦੇਖਦੇ ਏਹੁ ਹਰਿ ਕਾ ਰੂਪੁ ਹੈ ਹਰਿ ਰੂਪੁ ਨਦਰੀ ਆਇਆ ॥ "(GGS: 922). The saints sing God's glory and call God a wonderful Lord (*vaheguru* ਵਾਹਿਗੁਰੂ).

The creation of the universe is God's cosmic play. God is whole and the world in which we live is part of that whole. Sikh *gurus* emphasise the unity of God believing that God is the creator, sustainer and destroyer. God is all powerful and God's extent is infinite. Everything that happens in the universe is according to God's Divine Order (*hukam* - an Arabic word) and Will. This concept is frequently applied in *Guru Granth Sahib* to explain the nature of creation, universe and human life. Human life is understood to be a part of the Divine Order. It is a rich gift from God, something to be proud of and to be acknowledged. Birth and death occurs under God's Divine Order and are beyond the control of humans. Everything happens according to the Almighty's Will and nothing happens beyond Divine Orders. Therefore, it is the duty of a person to surrender and submit (*bhana manana* ਭਾਣਾ ਮੰਨਣਾ) to the Divine Will. Human beings are bestowed with the ability to distinguish right from wrong and good from evil. They can make their own destiny by performing good deeds. They will reap what they sow in their life; therefore, it is important for them to do good deeds, lead a truthful life and they should take care of God's creation.

God has created this universe and humans are the apex of this creation. They are the only ones privileged for spiritual attainment. Sikhism advocates family life and rejects asceticism in order to fulfil worldly responsibilities and render service towards humanity. One should remain detached from the materialistic world while fulfilling family responsibilities. Sikhism emphasises *kirt karo* (earning a living through honest and approved means), *wand chhako* (sharing with less fortunate, poor and needy) and *naam japo* (to recite the name of God) and above all *bhana manana* (accepting the Will of God). The ideal of a true Sikh is to look beyond the self and to serve one's fellow beings. It gives purpose and meaning to life. Realisation of God can be achieved by following virtuous qualities such as truth, righteousness, honesty, compassion, justice and humility.

It is believed in Sikhism that humans are God's own creation, and a divine spark called soul is added in a human body. Sikhism believes in the immortality of the soul as it is a part of God and beyond death or destruction. Human life is the final stage of the soul's progress to divinity. The soul enters bodily form according to an individual's actions (*karma*). It is important for human beings to do virtuous deeds and control the five evils- lust (ਕਾਮ kam), anger (ਕ੍ਰੋਧ krodh), greed (ਲੋਭ lobh), wordly love (ਮੋਹ moh) and ego (ਹੰਕਾਰ hankar) in order to nourish the soul.

Sikhism accepts the theory of *Karma* that human beings are punished or rewarded according to their actions and deeds. After death, a person is judged according to his/her actions and deeds. Any person with evil deeds goes into lower forms of life and goes through the chain transmigration (passage of the dead person's soul into another body after death - ਆਵਾਗਵਨ) and one who has done noble deeds gets a human life again. The concept of hell and heaven according to Sikhism is a mere hypothesis for clarifying the doctrine of *Karma*. Hell and heaven refer to the bad and good life which can be lived here and in earthly existence. In a way, hell and heaven are conditions of mind. A virtuous person is happy and contented, as if living in heaven whereas a wicked person is greedy and discontented, as if living in hell. The service of God's creation is the best way of working in harmony with the Divine Will. However, according to Sikhism, human beings earn God's grace by repentance, prayer and love which neutralise their previous karma.

2.0 The gender of God in Sikhism

This question on the gender of God according to Sikhism is often asked by inquirers. According to Sikh beliefs, God is beyond the cycle of birth and death, formless and timeless which deny any possibility of a specific gender. God belongs to neither sex if God is *ajuni* (ਅਜੂਨੀ) unborn. Though God is often referred as 'He' and the pronoun 'He' has been applied when referring to 'Oankar' yet God has no particular gender in Sikhism. God in the Sikh Scripture is referred to by several names mainly attributive and action related. Sikh *gurus* remembered God by addressing God with different human bonds like mother, father, kin and brother ਤੂੰ ਮੇਰਾ ਪਿਤਾ ਤੂੰ ਹੈ ਮੇਰਾ ਮਾਤਾ॥ ਤੂੰ ਮੇਰਾ ਬੰਧਪ ਤੂੰ ਮੇਰਾ ਭ੍ਰਾਤਾ॥ (GGS: 103). Other names expressive of God's supremacy are *thakur, prabhu, swami, patshah*. Some traditional names are *Ram, Rahim, Narayan, Allah* and *Khuda*. Guru Granth Sahib contains many names for God both masculine and feminine.

3.0 The place of Gurus in Sikhism

Guru means a religious teacher and a guide who is to be consulted, not to be worshipped. In Sikhism *gurus* are teachers and Sikhs are their disciples. A *Guru* is neither a prophet nor a messenger but a trusted servant sent to the world to encourage righteousness and to uproot evil. A *Guru's* message gives light. In Sikh theology, *Guru* is used for the ten *gurus* and the *gur-shabad* (word *guru*). Sikh *gurus* preached their message to masses irrespective of their colour, caste, creed and status. They recorded what they preached in the *Guru Granth Sahib* and this Holy Scripture was consecrated as *Guru*. It is the living embodiment of the ten *gurus*. The tenth *guru* Gobind Singh directed Sikhs to accept *Guru Granth Sahib* as their living *Guru*. After the tenth *guru*, it became the ultimate *Guru* of Sikhs. *Gurbani* is invariably called *shabad* and word. "Word" is the embodiment of eternal and changeless truth. The fundamental truth remains the same for all times. For Sikhs, there is no need of a physical *guru*.

4.0 Summary

Sikhism accepts the existence of God and believes in monotheism, that there is one and only one God, who is supreme and all pervading, formless, timeless and beyond the cycle of life and death. It emphasises the unity of God suggesting that God is creator, sustainer and destroyer. Nobody knows the extent of God and it is beyond human comprehension. Everything happens according to God's Divine Order and Will. Humanity is a rich gift from God and part of God's own creation. God put a divine spark and immortal soul in the human body. It is the duty of a person to surrender and submit to God's Divine

Will. Human beings are judged and rewarded according to their *karma* and get the next life based on their actions and deeds in this life. Sikhs believe in the process of chain transmigration (passage of the dead person's soul into another body after death) which means those with noble deeds get human form and others will get lower forms depending on their deeds. Sikhs do not believe in hell and heaven. It is a mere hypothesis for clarifying the doctrine of *Karma*. God has no specific gender and is addressed with different attributive and action related names and human relations by God's devotees and worshippers. *Guru* according to Sikhism is a teacher and a guide and Sikhs are disciples. For Sikhs, there is no need of a physical *guru*. After the tenth *guru, Guru Granth Sahib* became the ultimate *Guru* of Sikhs and they were told to accept the 'Word' as their *Guru*.

Chapter 4

Origin of the Universe, Environment and Ecology in Sikhism

1.0 Origin of the universe

The origin of the universe has always been an interesting and curious subject. There are opinions from scientists and from a faith perspective. According to Sikhism the universe is God's creation as it is mentioned in the Holy Scripture of Sikhs: ਖਾਕੁ ਨੂਰ ਕਰਦੰ ਆਲਮ ਦੁਨੀਆਇ ॥ ਅਸਮਾਨ ਜਿਮੀ ਦਰਖਤ ਆਬ ਪੈਦਾਇਸਿ ਖੁਦਾਇ ॥੧॥ (GGS: 723) which means 'The Lord infused His Light into the dust, and created the world, the universe. The sky, the earth, the trees, and the water - all are the creation of God.

It is also mentioned in the Holy Book that God existed all alone before the creation of the universe. God was in the state of pre-creation, a state of contemplation of the void (sunn Samadhi - ਸੁੰਨ ਸਮਾਧੀ). According to Guru Nanak, there was darkness and chaos for millions of years. There were mists and clouds. There was no day and night. There was also no sky, no moon and no sun. Nothing existed except God ਅਰਬਦ ਨਰਬਦ ਧੁੰਧੂਕਾਰਾ ॥ ਧਰਣਿ ਨ ਗਗਨਾ ਹੁਕਮੁ ਅਪਾਰਾ ॥ ਨਾ ਦਿਨੁ ਰੈਨਿ ਨ ਚੰਦ ਸੂਰਜੁ ਸੁੰਨ ਸਮਾਧਿ ਲਗਾਇਦਾ (GGS: 1035).

Further descriptions of the universe and its creation in Sikh Scripture are remarkably similar to recent scientific speculation about the universe and its origin. One of the basic hymns in the Sikh Scripture, which may be called the Hymn of the Genesis, describes the indeterminate void before the existence of this universe. The act of creation itself, the creation of the primeval atom, was instantaneous, caused by the Will of God.

Guru Nanak, the founder of the Sikh religion speaks of innumerable galaxies, of a limitless universe, the boundaries of which are beyond human ability to comprehend. God alone knows the extent of God's own creation. According to Sikh Scripture:

"Countless are the worlds beneath, countless are the worlds above.
No limit is found, nor have the Vedas.
Eighteen thousands, say the Semitic texts (This is not the last word).
Yea, the Essence alone is real.
He who counts doth fail in the deal.

Nanak: let us say, God is Great (God, the One).
The Almighty alone knows, yea, God alone.
ਪਾਤਾਲਾ ਪਾਤਾਲ ਲਖ ਆਗਾਸਾ ਅਗਾਸ॥ ਓੜਕ ਓੜਕ ਭਾਲਿ ਥਕੇ ਵੇਦ ਕਹਨਿ ਇਕ ਵਾਤ॥
ਸਹਸ ਅਠਾਰਹ ਕਹਨਿ ਕਤੇਬਾ ਅਸੁਲੂ ਇਕੁ ਧਾਤੁ॥ ਲੇਖਾ ਹੋਇ ਤ ਲਿਖੀਐ ਲੇਖੈ ਹੋਇ ਵਿਣਾਸੁ॥
ਨਾਨਕ ਵਡਾ ਆਖੀਐ ਆਪੇ ਜਾਣੈ ਆਪੁ॥ " (GGS: 5).

God created the universe and the world, for reasons best known to God. *Guru* Nanak declares that God alone knows the reasons for and the moment of the universe's creation. Its origin was in God and its end is in God, and it operates within God's Order/Will (*hukam* – ਹੁਕਮ). The world, like all creations, is a manifestation of God. Every creature in this world, every plant, every form is a manifestation of the Creator. Each is part of God and God is within each element of the creation. God is the cause of all and is also the primary connection between all God's existences.

Sikhism accepts the theory that God dwells in the human body. This is the microcosmic theory. The universe is the macrocosm, while the body is the microcosm, that is, the body is a miniature of the universe. *Guru* Amar Das puts it thus:

"Everything is in the body, the regions, the spheres and the nether worlds.
There are jewels in the body, there are stores of *Bhagti*.
There is the universe of nine regions within the body.
Brahma, Vishnu and Shiva reside in the body."

In the body, which is an epitome of the universe, resides the Lord of the universe. The devotee explores the body and finds hidden treasures therein. Ultimately a person finds God within his/her own self. God has not only created this world but has also provided each species and humans with means of support and nurturing.

2.0 Environment and ecology in Sikhism

Life of any kind, for its very existence and nurturing, depends upon a bounteous nature. A human being needs to derive sustenance from the earth. The creation of God has interconnection. For example a human body consists of many parts and all of them are dependent upon each other in spite of their different functions. Similarly all the constituents of this universe and this earth are dependent upon each other. They are part of the same system or order. The general belief is that things often go wrong when humans begin to interfere with nature. The choices made in one place have measurable consequences for the rest of the world because of the close proximity due to modern scientific inventions. The environment crisis at present is mainly caused by humanity's confrontation with nature and its exploitation of natural resources. It is leading to the depletion of renewable resources, destruction of forests, and overuse of land for agriculture and habitation. Today pollution is contaminating air, land, and water. Smoke from industry, homes, and vehicles is in the air. Industrial waste and consumer rubbish is affecting streams and rivers, ponds and lakes. Much of the waste is a product of modern technology which is not reusable and not biodegradable. Its long-term consequences are unknown. The viability of many animal and plant species, and possibly that of the human species itself, is at stake.

A human being needs to derive sustenance from the earth and not to deplete, exhaust, pollute, burn, or destroy it. This is necessary for the health of this planet and for human survival. *Guru* Amar Das, the third Sikh *guru* created a remedy centre by growing bushes and trees which can be used for medicinal purposes. The Sikh *gurus* advocated a simple lifestyle, which is environmentally friendly, for example smoking is not only unhealthy but also pollutes the air. They advocated maximising the use of resources and not to waste them. It is also suggested in Sikhism not to harm others (standing for social justice and fairness). Modern times have seen the use of modern warfare and nuclear testing resulting in enormous damage to the planet's ecology. Consequently climate change and weather has become unpredictable. There are floods, drought and natural calamities shattering the existence of many. All this is happening because of humans, in particularly scientists' intrusion into nature's territory. It is important to co-exist and not to interfere in the ways of nature.

The Holy Sikh Scripture has given a lot of importance to nature and its elements:

ਪਉਣੁ ਗੁਰੂ ਪਾਣੀ ਪਿਤਾ ਮਾਤਾ ਧਰਤਿ ਮਹਤੁ (GGS: 146)
This means Air is *Guru*, Water is the Father and Earth is the great Mother of all.

Guru, father and mother are respected therefore these elements are compared with these human relations so that they should be cared for and respected. The pollution of these elements is against the principles laid down by the Sikh *gurus*. The *Guru* says:

ਪਉਣ ਪਾਣੀ ਧਰਤੀ ਆਕਾਸੁ ਘਰ ਮੰਦਰ ਹਰਿ ਬਨੀ (GGS: 723) meaning air, water, earth and sky – the Lord has made these God's home and temple. Such sacred places need to be protected and looked after. Sikh *gurus* made many *gurdwaras* surrounded by large pools (*sarovar* or *baolis* - ਸਰੋਵਰ/ਬਾਉਲੀ). Even the *Gurbani* refers to various trees and other  species which are useful to people. The *Gurus* inferred that it is not the girth, size, or beautiful flowers that determine the significance of a tree but it is its usefulness that makes it important for mankind. Sikh religion has also given importance to vegetation indicated by sacred plantation in and around *gurdwaras* and their pools.

Sikhism teaches against a life of wasteful consumption. The environmental concerns may be viewed as part of the broader issue of human development and social justice. Many environmental problems, particularly the exploitation of environmental resources in developing nations, are due to poverty and wars for natural resources.

Sikhs believe in the environmental ethics dedicated to the awareness of the sacred relationship between humans and the environment. The Sikh gurus realised the significance of the environment and ecological balance from the very beginning. Sikh Scriptures teach us to care for the environment not in a mechanical way but through an attitude of love and well being of all '*sarbat da bhalla*'. In Sikh beliefs, a concern for the environment is part of the integrated approach to life and nature. As all creation has the same origin and end, humans must have consciousness of their place in creation and their relationship with it. It is necessary to preserve this relationship for the healthy existence of this planet.

3.0 Summary

The origin of the world is unknown and beyond the comprehension of human knowledge and ancient religious books. God existed all alone in the state of contemplation. There was darkness and chaos for millions of years. The universe was created with God's Order and there are many more worlds underneath and above this world. God resides within human beings and also in every element of God's own creation.

God's creation has one origin and end. Nature and human life is dependant upon each other for their existence and survival. Humans should learn to live in harmony with and not to confront nature. Sikh religion advocates caring for and maximising the use of natural resources. Natural elements have their own place in this planet and they are there for a reason and purpose. Intrusion by humans and scientists through modern technology into nature's territory has resulted in enormous damage to the environment and ecology bringing unpredictable changes in climate and weather. Sikh religion has made references to protect the environment and ecology. For example, smoking is prohibited in Sikhism not only for health reasons but also because of the pollution of the air.

Chapter 5
Equality and Sikhism

1.0 Equality

Equality is a key concept in the Sikh religion, and refers to caste, class and gender. Sikh teachings lay emphasis on all kinds of equality, placing a high value on human dignity. Promotion of equality and the rejection of the caste system and other symbols of inequality are part of Sikhism. Sikhism firmly advocates the equality of all people especially women.

Sikh ethics define doctrines of values in human conduct. It suggests some rules by which Sikhs should lead their life. The Code of Conduct has a profound impact on Sikh living. There are also references in the *Guru Granth Sahib* about equality stressing upon social justice, love for humanity, voluntary service and sharing with the less fortunate in order to create social equality. Social inequality can be examined within the context of caste inequality, relations among economic classes (class or social status), attitude towards other religions and the status of women in society. Guru Nanak's successors reiterated again and again this anti-caste sentiment.

1.1 Caste inequalities

The caste system was deeply ingrained within the Indian society for several thousand years before Guru Nanak and it was embedded in the social fabric of India as a way of determining social roles and occupations. It divided the community on the basis of higher and lower caste. Caste, originally founded on the basis of occupation, was later attached to birth and it was rigidly practiced in the Hindu society. Human beings were valued on the basis of their caste rather than their deeds. It was this social hierarchy that Guru Nanak repudiated. He rejected the notion that status ascribed by birth determines the rank of humans and viewed differences based on birth as irrelevant to the sanctity of the individual. *Guru* Nanak taught there was one God and one creation, and that inherited differences have no meaning in the relationship between humans and God. *Guru* Nanak also denied the accepted dogma that only higher castes could achieve spiritual liberation.

There were four castes ranking *Brahmans* (priests) as highest, *Kshatriyas* (warriors) the next, *Vaishyas* (traders) the third and the *Shudras* (menial workers) the lowest of all. The Sikh *gurus* tried to create an equal society based on human dignity. According to *Guru* Amar Das:

"All say there are four castes
But God creates one and all...
The five elements make up the body
And nobody can say who has less or more
ਚਾਰੇ ਵਰਨ ਆਖੈ ਸਭ ਕੋਈ ॥ ਬ੍ਰਹਮ ਬਿੰਦ ਤੇ ਸਭ ਓਪਤਿ ਹੋਈ ॥ ੨ ॥
ਮਾਟੀ ਏਕ ਸਗਲ ਸੰਸਾਰਾ ॥ ਬਹੁ ਬਿਧਿ ਭਾਂਡੇ ਘੜੇ ਕੁਮਾਰਾ ॥ ੩ ॥
ਪੰਚ ਤਤੁ ਮਿਲਿ ਦੇਹੀ ਕਾ ਆਕਾਰਾ ॥ ਘਟਿ ਵਧਿ ਕੋ ਕਰੈ ਬੀਚਾਰਾ ॥ ੪ ॥" (GGS:1128)

The tenth Sikh *guru*, Gobind Singh, furthered the principle of equality by establishing the order of the *Khalsa* and declared caste to be a hindrance to the unity of the *Khalsa*. The first five members of the Khalsa came from different caste backgrounds, and three were from lower castes. Though their caste ranking was mixed, *Guru* Gobind Singh asked them to drink from the same bowl, an act contrary to caste pollution rules. He also instituted the practice of giving all Sikh men the suffix of '*Singh*' (lion) to their names and all Sikh women '*Kaur*' (lioness/princess). This is significant for Sikhs as the suffix of *Singh* and *Kaur* not only brings them within the fold of the *Khalsa Panth* (religious order) but is also indicative of bravery. Furthermore, Sikhs are instructed not to use their caste as part of their names in order to create an equal society. *Guru* Gobind Singh created *Khalsa Panth*, saint soldiers who could fight against oppression and injustice in order to establish equality. The tenth *guru*, Gobind Singh, brought equality between the *guru* and the disciple by initiating five men and bringing them into the *Khalsa* fold through an initiation ceremony and then getting initiated himself through these five Sikhs. This relationship between guru and disciple was also based on equality.

All the Sikh *gurus* have been strong supporters of equality and all of them rejected the caste based discrimination. God's light (soul) is within all creatures and there is no difference between the souls of humans. All belong to the one human race.

"Your light is the light in all beings, O Creator.
Your entire expanse is true.
ਸਭ ਜੋਤਿ ਤੇਰੀ ਜੋਤੀ ਵਿਚਿ ਕਰਤੇ ਸਭੁ ਸਚੁ ਤੇਰਾ ਪਾਸਾਰਾ ॥" (GGS: 1314).

In addition,

"Recognise the Lord's Light within all, and do not consider social class or status
There are no classes or castes in the world hereafter.
ਜਾਣਹੁ ਜੋਤਿ ਨ ਪੂਛਹੁ ਜਾਤੀ ਆਗੈ ਜਾਤਿ ਨ ਹੇ ॥" (GGS 349).

The *gurus* made every attempt possible to break down the caste barriers. The early Sikh *gurus* established the tradition of a free community kitchen called *Langar*. In this practice, any person regardless of caste, class or social status eats together  sitting side by side in a row *(pangat)*. *Langar* is prepared by volunteers and served in all *gurdwaras* reminding Sikhs of the importance and significance of human equality. The practices introduced by Sikh *gurus* affirm that caste discrimination has no place in modern Sikh society or Sikh ceremonies.

The Holy Scripture of Sikhs includes the hymns written by Ravidas, a leather worker, and hymns by Kabir, a Muslim weaver. Both poets made a significant contribution to the *Guru Granth Sahib* despite their social standing in the community. The Sikh beliefs that all humans are of one form and one God has made them all leave no space for discriminatory practices.

1.2 Economic (class or social status) inequalities

The Sikh religion promotes a classless society, giving more importance to virtue than wealth. The status of an individual should be determined by deeds or merits, not by class or social position. All should be treated as equal, irrespective of their material resources. According to *Guru* Nanak:

"One lives not ever in the world:
Neither king nor beggars would remain, they all come and go.
ਰਾਜੇ ਰਾਇ ਰੰਕ ਨਹੀ ਰਹਣਾ ਆਇ ਜਾਇ ਜੁਗ ਚਾਰੇ ॥ " (GGS: 931).

Guru Arjan Dev said:
"The wisdom of God looks upon all alike,
such as the wind that blows alike for the commoner and the king.
ਬ੍ਰਹਮਗਿਆਨੀ ਕੈ ਦ੍ਰਿਸਟਿ ਸਮਾਨਿ ॥
ਜੈਸੇ ਰਾਜ ਰੰਕ ਕਉ ਲਗੈ ਤੁਲਿ ਪਵਾਨ ॥ " (GGS: 272).

In the same paragraph, the *Guru* alludes to nature and asserts that:

"Just as nature treats all alike, in the similar way, the wise in God treats all alike.
ਬ੍ਰਹਮ ਗਿਆਨੀ ਕਉ ਇਹੈ ਗੁਨਾਉ ॥
ਨਾਨਕ ਜਿਉ ਪਾਵਕ ਕਾ ਸਹਜ ਸੁਭਾਉ ॥ ".

Guru Nanak accepted the hospitality of *Bhai* Lalo, a poor, honest and hard working artisan rather than the rich man of the same village thus demonstrating the valuing of honest earning and living. The Sikh *gurus* regarded the rich and poor equal. Preference was not given to the wealthy but to the virtuous.

1.3 Gender inequality

At the time of *Guru* Nanak in the 15th century, Indian women were severely degraded and oppressed. They were treated unfairly for centuries. The caste system, economic oppression, denial of property rights and inheritance, a false sense of impurity attached to menstruation and child birth, deliberate deprivation of education led to the deterioration of women's position in society. Given no education or freedom to make decisions, their presence in religious, political, social, cultural, and economic affairs was virtually non-existent. Women were referred to as seducers and distractions from man's spiritual path, unclean, and as temptresses. They were denied the right to preach or to participate in religious rites.

The structure of Indian society was patriarchal (male head of the family) and this was reinforced and perpetuated in the name of religion. Religions at that time condoned the inferior status of women. In general, the condition of women was humiliating. They were considered to be inferior and the property of their fathers, husbands and sons. Their function was only to bear children, do household work, and serve the male members of their families. Men were allowed to practice polygamy (having more than one wife), but women widowers were not even allowed to remarry. In some parts of India, they were encouraged to commit *sati* (committing suicide by throwing themselves onto their dead husband's funeral pyre) and were sometimes even forced to. Child marriage and female infanticide (the killing of girls at birth) were practiced. Veiling (*purdah*) was common among women in north India. They did not participate in public life but generally remained secluded in the home.

The Sikh *gurus* condemned unethical practices prevalent at that time and took a firm stand against derogatory practices as regards to the status of women. They introduced the concept of gender equality which applied equally to both men and women in all spheres of life. This was promoted through the teachings and practices of the Sikh *gurus*. Sikh teachings also give women full equality to participate in religious performances, to be equal partners in marriage and family life and, if the need arises, to participate in warfare making a full contribution to the secular and religious life.

The status of a woman is clearly defined in Sikhism. Sikh *gurus*, in particular, emphasised gender equality, giving full and equal status to women. The vision of the *gurus* on this matter was far ahead of their time. The authoritative work on this subject is the *Guru Granth Sahib*, supported by the words and practices of the Sikh *gurus* and the Sikh Code of Conduct (*Rahitnama*-ਰਹਿਤਨਾਮਾ). There are a number of hymns in the *Guru Granth Sahib* to support these concepts and the *gurus* introduced practical measures to achieve what they preached.

Sikh *gurus* moulded traditional lifestyles to exemplify a more equitable society. They created institutions that formed the basis of human equality.

2.0 Sikh ideology and the status of women

The Sikh *gurus* adopted a two-fold approach to gender issues. They took a positive attitude towards women in order to enhance their status and prestige. They also condemned the practices prevalent in Indian society, which undermined women. *Guru* Nanak, the first Sikh *guru*, condemned the man-made notion of the inferiority of women and he argued for their liberation. The spirit of the Sikh woman was raised with the belief that she was not a helpless creature but a responsible being endowed with a will of her own, with which she could do much to mould the destiny of society.

He declared that women must be respected as they were the source of humanity's physical existence and of its entire social life.

"It is by woman, the 'condemned' one that we are conceived and from her that we are born; it is with her that we are betrothed and married.
It is the woman we befriend; it is she who keeps the race going.
When one woman dies, we seek another; it is with her that we become established in society.
ਭੰਡਿ ਜੰਮੀਐ ਭੰਡਿ ਨਿੰਮੀਐ ਭੰਡਿ ਮੰਗਣੁ ਵੀਆਹੁ ॥
ਭੰਡਹੁ ਹੋਵੈ ਦੋਸਤੀ ਭੰਡਹੁ ਚਲੈ ਰਾਹੁ ॥
ਭੰਡੁ ਮੁਆ ਭੰਡੁ ਭਾਲੀਐ ਭੰਡਿ ਹੋਵੈ ਬੰਧਾਨੁ ॥ " (GGS: 473)

"Why should we call her 'inferior'?
Who gives birth to kings?
ਸੋ ਕਿਉ ਮੰਦਾ ਆਖੀਐ ਜਿਤੁ ਜੰਮਹਿ ਰਾਜਾਨ ॥ " (GGS: 473)

In the *Guru Granth Sahib*, a woman receives great veneration in Sikh society as "she gives birth to kings and divines" (GGS: 473). As a mother, she receives the respect of the whole society and as a wife she is the better half of her husband. She keeps the world going and she is the bond of family and social life. From this Scriptural authority, it is clear that women are given a high position in the Sikh society.

2.1 Women in Sikh religion and religious practices

Guru Nanak denounced the idea that spirituality was only for men, and not for women. The first Sikh *guru* in his preaching and writings made direct statements emphasising that women were no less than men. The Sikh *gurus* invited women to join the *sangat* (congregation) and work with men in the *langar* (communal kitchen). Sikhism allowed women full participation in religious activities. *Guru Amar Das*, the third Sikh *guru* appointed 52 women missionaries out of 146 to spread the Sikh message and, out of 22 *manjis* (dioceses) established by the *Guru* for the preaching of Sikhism, 4 were headed by women. The contribution of sugar crystal (*patasha*-ਪਤਾਸਾ) in the preparation of baptismal water (*Amrit*-ਅੰਮ੍ਰਿਤ) by the wife of the tenth *guru* was also an indication of the participation of women in religious matters. Guru Gobind Singh opened up the initiation ceremony to both men and women. Following the efforts of the Sikh *gurus*, women could join and lead the holy congregations, take part in the recitation of the Holy Scripture, work as *granthis* (ਗ੍ਰੰਥੀ) and as preachers. Sikhism also states that both men and women are capable of reaching the highest levels of spirituality.

"In all beings is He Himself pervasive, Himself pervades all forms, male or female ਸਭਿ ਘਟ ਆਪੇ ਭੋਗਵੈ ਪਿਆਰਾ ਵਿਚਿ ਨਾਰੀ ਪੁਰਖੁ ਸਭੁ ਸੋਇ ॥ " (GGS: 605)

The idea of abstaining from the worldly comforts and pleasures (*sanyasa*-ਸੰਨਿਆਸਾ) had influenced attitudes towards women in India. The inherent attraction of the female was considered to be a temptation, something against which the *sanyasi* must be warned and to which he must not be attracted. The *gurus* did not regard women as hurdles or obstructions on the path to salvation. They rejected the idea of asceticism or renunciation (*sanyas*-ਸੰਨਿਆਸ) and regarded the family life, if it was led in a righteous manner, to be superior to that of the ascetic. In order to emphasise the superiority of the householder's life, the Sikh *gurus* placed great emphasis on marriage and family life. Polygamy was disapproved in Sikhism and only monogamous marriage was believed to fit Sikh values. The *gurus* expected that women would be given honourable status in every segment of society. Thus, according to Sikh theology, she was declared not inferior to man and having equal responsibility for her actions before God.

2.2 Socio-religious traditions

Sikhism suggested practical steps for the equality of women with men. At the emergence of Sikhism, certain practices involving women were prevalent, such as *sati*, female infanticide, and the wearing of the veil, thus undermining women in society. The *gurus* condemned traditions that demeaned the position of women and created practices to ensure equal and respectable status for them.

Female infanticide was a common practice in medieval India. The main reasons for the practice were superstition, the expense of the dowry for daughters and the difficulty of finding suitable husbands. The Sikh *gurus* denounced such practices and also offered solutions for their causes. It was further added that those indulging in female infanticide were to be excommunicated from Sikhism, and those having any social relations with them were deemed punishable (Sikh *Rahit Maryada*: 23, xi).

Sikhism advocated discarding the dowry system. Concerning dowry, Guru Ram Das states:

"All other dowry displayed by the self-willed is false egoism and a vain show. O my father, bless me with the dowry of the Lord's Name
ਹੋਰਿ ਮਨਮੁਖਿ ਦਾਜੁ ਜਿ ਰਖਿ ਦਿਖਾਲਹਿ ਸੁ ਕੂੜੁ ਅਹੰਕਾਰੁ ਕਚੁ ਪਾਜੋ ॥
ਹਰਿ ਪ੍ਰਭ ਮੇਰੇ ਬਾਬੁਲਾ ਹਰਿ ਦੇਵਹੁ ਦਾਨੁ ਮੈ ਦਾਜੋ ॥੪॥" (GGS: 79)

"No dowry ought to be accepted from the bride's parents" (Sikh *Rahit Maryada*: 28, xii). On the contrary, social help should be offered to parents experiencing difficulty in finding a match for their daughter and also in arranging her marriage.

Sati refers to a faithful wife and a chaste woman who voluntarily burns herself alive on her husband's funeral pyre. It was believed that this action would expiate the sins of three generations and would obtain for a woman the posthumous title of *sati*. This hope and encouragement was used to induce women to kill themselves while there was no such requirement for a man on the death of his wife. The Sikh *gurus* rejected this custom and Guru Amar Das declared, "*Sati* is one who lives contented and embellishes herself with good conduct and cherishes the Lord for ever and calls on Him. ਭੀ ਸੋ ਸਤੀਆ ਜਾਣੀਅਨਿ ਸੀਲ ਸੰਤੋਖਿ ਰਹੰਨਿ॥ ਸੇਵਨਿ ਸਾਈ ਆਪਣਾ ਨਿਤ ਉਠਿ ਸੰਮਾਲੰਨਿ॥" (GGS: 787). The virtue of a woman lay in the role she played in the family and not in her death. The *gurus* also allowed female widows to remarry.

The custom of veiling (*purdah*-ਪਰਦਾ) came to the Punjab with Islam. *Purdah* was a form of covering, which took different forms such as the body cover (*burkah*-ਬੁਰਕਾ), the shawl (*chadar*-ਚਾਦਰ) and the face covering (*ghund*-ਘੁੰਡ). It was a custom strictly enforced upon women, as a protection against the lustful eyes of men. The gurus disapproved the custom of covering the face in whatever form and stated that women ought not to be veiled. *Guru* Amar Das was the first to condemn *purdah*. He believed it was demeaning for women. The immediate effect of the removal of *purdah* was that the spirit of a woman was raised with a belief that she was not a helpless creature but was responsible for defending her own honour and dignity.

All human beings, regardless of gender, caste, race, status or birth are judged only by their deeds. Equality is the very basis of Sikhism. Sikhism values human dignity and importance is given to human actions and not to class, position and status. Similarly they treated oppressed and down trodden people with respect providing equality and advocating social justice.

3.0 Sikh attitude towards other religions

Sikhism believes in human equality and gives respect to other religions. All human beings are God's creation and no one is high or low. They are judged and valued by their deeds. Religion guides humans to do right things and motivates towards attaining a high moral and spiritual life. No religion is inferior or superior. Sikhism advocates respecting all religions and expects adherents of other religions to be sincere and dedicated to their own religion. Sikhs believe in one God and lead their life according to the principles and teachings of their *gurus* and *Guru Granth Sahib*. Sikhs should live in peace and harmony but it is against Sikh principles to tolerate any kind of oppression. They are allowed to use force in order to get justice if all other peaceful means fail. Sikhism is against fanaticism and forcible conversion. Sikh *gurus* sacrificed their life for religious freedom. There are references and discourses found on the merits of those believing in religions other than Sikhism. The inclusion of the compositions of saints of other religions such as Farid, a Muslim mystic (*sufi* poet) and Kabir, a Muslim weaver in the Holy Book confirms that the Sikh religion has an open approach towards other religions. *Guru* Gobind Singh proclaimed, "God is in the Hindu temple as well as in the mosque. God is addressed in both the Hindu and the Muslim prayer; all people are one though they appear different and have different habits under the influence of different environments. All are made of five elements. The *Qur'an* and the *Puranas* praise the same God. They are all of one form and one God has made them all" (*Guru* Gobind Singh, *Akal Ustat*: 86). Sikhs believe that because God is present in every person, each person stands as an equal before God, regardless of ethnicity, creed, colour, nationality or gender. Sikhism stands for respect, freedom of conscience and social equality. It promotes religious, spiritual and social freedom of all beings.

4.0 Summary

Complete equality among all is declared as the fundamental moral principle by the Sikh *gurus*. The validity of the caste inequality is denied as there is no fundamental difference among people with all our differences in terms of physical constitution and laws of nature. The spiritual realisation can be attained by anyone with noble deeds.

Wealth is also a determinant of social classes besides the caste system. The Sikh religion rejects distinctions based on ownership of economic resources. The practical initiatives taken by Sikh *gurus* are indicative of the strong belief in equality. *Langar* is representative of an acknowledgment of social equality and integration. The tenth *guru* created *Khalsa* (pure ones) by bringing people from different occupations and backgrounds and binding them in an order called *Khalsa Panth* through an initiation ceremony. He also brought equality between the *guru* and the disciple by initiating five men and then getting initiated himself through these five Sikhs. Sikh *gurus* tried to revolutionise the society which treated women and the social outcast worse than animals.

Sikhism was a progressive religion well ahead of its time when it was founded in the 15th Century. Sikhs are enjoined by sacred ideals to assert a high standard of human equality, and be models of fairness and respect. Gender equality was the very basis of Sikhism. Women were allowed to participate in all walks of life and *gurus* raised their voice against the meaningless traditions undermining women and their status in the society. In the Sikh faith, there is no basis for discrimination in regard to caste, race, gender, religion or socioeconomic standing. There is no superior and inferior but the actions of people determine their place in society. The principle of human equality is an integral part of the Sikh Scripture and lived traditions. The compositions of the *Guru Granth Sahib* exhibit this non-discriminatory policy by including the hymns of saints of other religions and lower classes. To demean someone on the basis of colour, creed, gender, or ethnic origin is contrary to the spirit of Sikhism and the visions of the Sikh *gurus*.

Chapter 6

Family Life

1.0 Family life

Sikh teachings stress the importance of the institution of marriage and family life. It is recognised that living within a family promotes a pious life. Renunciation or celibacy is not favoured by Sikhism.

"Why go out to search God in the woods?
For, though ever Detached, He abides within us all: Yea, He also Lives within thee
ਕਾਹੇ ਰੇ ਬਨ ਖੋਜਨ ਜਾਈ ॥
ਸਰਬ ਨਿਵਾਸੀ ਸਦਾ ਅਲੇਪਾ ਤੋਹੀ ਸੰਗਿ ਸਮਾਈ ॥" (GGS: 684).

Salvation in Sikhism can not be attained by renunciation but it can be achieved by living in a family, earning one's living by honest means, sharing with the poor and needy and meditating on the name of God. Family in Sikhism is not only husband and wife and their children but refers to joint and extended family. Joint and extended families were the norm in the Punjab though it is changing now because people are moving away from villages for one reason or another. The essence of joint family living is still ingrained in many Sikh minds i.e. to help family members in their need be it financial or moral support and also to respect the older members of their families. It is a duty of every Sikh to care for their parents and give their children a good upbringing. Parents should be respected and looked after in their old age. The concept of *seva* (voluntary service) is important in Sikhism and this starts from home and extends to the wider community. It is suggested that a Sikh should remain detached to materialistic things while performing his/her family responsibilities.

2.0 Marriage

The *gurus* advocated marriage and family life. The institution of marriage is given importance and even priests are allowed to marry according to Sikhism. The Sikh *gurus* went to the extent of saying if a suitable match is not found, help the parents to find one and support them in organising the wedding. Marriage rather than being a union of bodies, is held to be a union of souls, of minds, leading to love of one another's qualities and care for each other's well being. The marriage relationship as mere sexual gratification was also condemned. The couple should be well matched. *Guru* Amar Das states:

"They are not said to be husband and wife who merely sit together. Rather they alone are called husband and wife, who have one soul in two bodies.

ਧਨ ਪਿਰੁ ਏਹਿ ਨ ਆਖੀਅਨਿ ਬਹਨਿ ਇਕਠੇ ਹੋਇ॥

ਏਕ ਜੋਤਿ ਦੁਇ ਮੂਰਤੀ ਧਨ ਪਿਰ ਕਹੀਐ ਸੋਇ॥" (GGS: 788).

The Sikh religion favours compatible marriages suggesting one light in two bodies (ਏਕ ਜੋਤਿ ਦੋਇ ਮੂਰਤੀ). A Sikh should marry a Sikh according to *Sikh Rahit Maryada*. Marriage to other religions is not approved and frowned upon in spite of the fact that there is no evidence to support this in the *Guru Granth Sahib*. This might be suggested for practical reasons keeping in view that the commonality of culture and religion may help to make a lasting marriage. Sikhs can have inter-caste marriage within their own religion as caste system is condemned in Sikh religion. Child marriage is also condemned in Sikhism and it is suggested that one should only marry when one is mature and able to take family responsibilities.

Sikhism does not prescribe to any particular type of marriage such as arranged or self chosen. Educated women are keen for compatibility, which they consider essential for a successful personal and professional life. They prefer to choose their own partners. Arranged marriage has been a tradition in the Punjab because of its cultural influence not because of religious dictate. Therefore, this became a norm in the Sikh community. In the case of an arranged marriage, the parents look for a partner for their son or daughter. The marriage is arranged not only with the consent and approval of both families but also the agreement of both bride and bridegroom. An arranged marriage does not mean forcing a boy or a girl into wedlock of the parents' choice only. There is general confusion between arranged and forced marriages. Sikhs can choose their own partners. There is no religious dictate as to whether one must choose this way or that way. Mostly it is considered best that the life partner is chosen with the consent of all parties.

Guru Hargobind, the sixth *guru* said that a wife was the conscience of a man (*aurat iman hai*-ਔਰਤ ਇਮਾਨ ਹੈ). She should act as a check and restraint on his weaknesses. Sikhism allows remarriage of a widow or widower and it is often encouraged if it happens at a young age.

The *gurus* redefined celibacy as marriage to one wife and taught that male and female should practice marital fidelity. This implies that they should be dedicated and loyal to each other. The practice of having more than one wife would run counter to the spirit of equality between the sexes. Only monogamous marriage was believed to fit Sikh values. Extra marital relations are forbidden. The ideal family is one where there is harmony and understanding. The status given to a wife is equal to her husband and she is not considered inferior in any way. She should be respected and not treated as a man's property and a carer for his family.

Most importantly, a marriage should be simple, and it should be performed in front of *Guru Granth Sahib* in the presence of the bride and bridegroom's families and *sangat* (congregation).

2.1 Dowry

The Sikh religion condemns the dowry, though it is prevalent in the Sikh community. Sikhs refer to dowry as '*daaj*'. Dowry, as applied to the Sikh community in the Punjab, is the tradition of giving gifts or presents to the daughter by her parents on the occasion of her marriage at the time of her leaving the parental home. These gifts and presents usually conform to social norms of the time and are normally followed as a guide as what to give to their daughters in marriage. Wealthy families do not restrict themselves to the prevailing social norms. They try to reflect their wealth in the amount of dowry they give to their daughters. Dowry is always generous, because it is a status confirmer and much talked about within the community. It normally consists of four components. The first component consists of items of clothing for the bride; suits of clothing and *sarees*. The second component of *daaj* is gold given to the bride from her family. The third part consists of household goods, including utensils, crockery, kitchen gadgets, linen, quilts, furniture and items such as sewing machines, washing machines, dishwashers and stereos. The fourth component relates to the gifts received by the groom's family and close relations. The main recipients are the groom and his parents.

Dowry is not demanded or asked for in the Sikh community, but it has become obligatory. Dowry is given by the 'bride givers' without expecting a return, and it is the 'bride takers' right to be the recipients. The Sikh concept of dowry is different from some other parts of India where the amount of dowry and cash is fixed before settling the marriage date and the marriage does not take place unless that fixed dowry and sum is paid. The fundamental difference is that no money is asked for in the dowry and generally no dowry is fixed in marriage transactions. In spite of this, a dowry may be a sign of affection but it can also be a burden for those parents who can not afford to comply with the social norms. This custom is widely practiced in Punjab and is also continued by Sikhs wherever they have settled. In fact the amount of dowry has increased with the growing earning capacity of Sikh women. Sikhs are forbidden from marrying off their children for monetary benefit, suggesting neither a woman nor a man should be married for money.

2.2 Divorce

Sikh marriage (*Anand karaj*) is regarded as a spiritual relationship performed in front of *Guru Granth Sahib* which binds the couple for their lifetime. Therefore, there is no scope for divorce or the breaking of the bond established in the presence of the *Granth Sahib*. Further more, the *Anand* Marriage Act 1909 gave a wife status equal to that of her husband. Under this Act, no provision was made for a divorce considering a marriage was a permanent relationship between the partners. Therefore, Sikhs have no personal law to this effect. However they are covered under the Hindu Code or the Civil Marriage Act which provides for divorce for Hindus, including Sikhs passed by the Indian parliament in 1955. For diasporas, it is natural that the law of the country where they settled applies. Generally, grounds like cruelty, adultery, change of religion, suffering from an incurable disease and in some, incompatibility of temperaments are accepted by courts for purposes of divorce. Divorcees according to Sikhism can and are allowed to remarry.

2.3 Family planning

Family planning in Sikhism is not discussed openly. There are certain issues which may not be pressing at the time and they hardly get mentioned. The *gurus* told their followers to exercise self-control and to regulate sex sensibly. The *gurus* recommended the middle way between self indulgence and abstinence. Similarly, there is no injunction in Sikhism against the use of contraceptives. Sikhs can practice family planning by using modern methods or through self-restraint if necessary. Life is regarded as a gift of God and is most sacred in Sikh teachings. Abortion is forbidden as it is interference in the creative work of God and also does not comply with accepting the Will of God. If the conception has taken place, it is a sin to destroy life and hence deliberate miscarriage or abortion is not approved of. Similarly, experimenting with embryos and foetus aborting is discouraged. Aborting a foetus is a modern form of female infanticide. Sikh *gurus* condemned female infanticide in their times and it is also condemned in the Sikh Code of Conduct. There are clear instructions that one who kills female infants, has no place in Sikh society, and has to be excommunicated. The birth of a girl or boy should be equally joyous for Sikhs.

It is best to use a common sense approach to family planning according to one's circumstances. It may become necessary in the case of the upbringing of existing children or ill health of the partner where medical advice needs to take priority and should be followed. Family planning, use of contraceptives, homosexual relations, lesbian and gay marriages are not referred to in the Sikh Scripture as they may not have been an issue at the time of their writing.

3.0 Euthanasia or mercy killing

The Sikh attitude towards euthanasia or mercy killing is quite clear. It has no place in Sikhism. Humans are supposed to accept the God's Will. The *gurus* regarded suffering a result of *karma* (action or deeds). One must have the moral courage to bear one's suffering without lament. One should pray for the grace of God to enable one to accept pain in a spirit of resignation and surrender. Life and death is the prerogative of God. The *gurus* tackled the problem of sickness and suffering by providing medical relief and alleviation of pain. Similarly suicide is also not allowed in Sikhism as it is interference in God's plan.

4.0 Summary

Family life is very important in Sikhism and the emphasis is given to the institution of marriage. Renunciation is condemned and Sikhs are encouraged to live in a family and they are advised to detach themselves from materialism. In the family there should be love and harmony in the relationship of husband and wife. Elderly parents should be respected and cared for and the children should be loved and given a good upbringing. Marriage according to Sikhism is a sacrament and not a civil contract. It takes place in front of *Guru Granth Sahib* binding a couple in a permanent relationship. Marriage across caste is permitted since caste system is condemned in the Sikh religion. Inter religious marriage is disapproved of by the Sikh Code of Conduct though there is no reference regarding this in the Holy Scripture. Sikhs are not supposed to give or take dowry. Child marriage is prohibited. Priests are allowed to marry according to Sikhism. Divorcees, widows or widowers are allowed to remarry. Family planning, use of contraceptives, homosexual relations, lesbian and gay marriages are not referred to in the Sikh Scripture as it may not have been an issue at the time of their writing. Abortion and female infanticide are not approved. Mercy killing is also disapproved of by Sikhism on the basis that suffering and pain are the result of one's actions and deeds.

Chapter 7
Sikh Ceremonies and Festivals

1.0 Sikh ceremonies

Religion is an integral part of Sikh life from birth until death. The Sikh life cycle rites of birth, naming, marriage and death have a special significance for the Sikh community and are closely associated with religion. These ceremonies are performed in the *gurdwara* in front of the *Guru Granth Sahib* in the presence of family, relatives, friends and congregation (*sangat*).

1.1 Birth

The birth of a child is considered to be a blessing from God. When a child is born, a naming ceremony is held in the *gurdwara* a few weeks after the birth. This is the first visit at which the child and the family receive religious blessings. Practically all children receive their name in this traditional manner. When the mother is well enough, the family will visit the *gurdwara*. Every child receives a name made up of two elements: the first element of the name is determined by the process in which the *granthi* opens the *Guru Granth Sahib*. The name of the child is taken from the first letter of the *vak* (first word of the passage of the *Guru Granth Sahib* read after its random opening) from the left hand page and this is read to the parents. They will then decide upon a name beginning with the first letter and the *granthi* will announce it publicly, adding the suffix of *Kaur* (lioness/princesses) for a girl and *Singh* (lion) for a boy. *Guru* Gobind Singh aimed to create saint soldiers who could fight against oppression and this suffix reminds Sikhs of their duty. This adding of a suffix with their given name brings them within the Sikh fold. Adding a surname is against the principles of Sikhism as it indicates caste or position in the society and such indications are against the principles of equality.

1.2 Marriage

The Sikh marriage is known as *Anand karaj* (*Anand* means bliss and *karaj* means ceremony). In Sikhism, marriage is a sacrament and not a civil contract. It takes place in front of *Guru Granth Sahib* thus establishing a permanent relationship between the partners.

Chapter 7 — Sikh Ceremonies and Festivals

Sikh marriages are performed according to guru-maryada (compulsory rituals in the presence of the *Guru Granth Sahib*). Any *amritdhari* Sikh (man or woman who has undergone traditional initiation and therefore practices the prescribed Sikh code of conduct in daily life) can perform a marriage ceremony. They follow a definite pattern which applies to all Sikhs. The two obligatory rituals are the *karmai* (the engagement) and *viah* (the wedding ceremony). Engagement takes place before the wedding and it must be done according to Sikh religion. This religious ceremony should be performed for all Sikh weddings. The marriage ceremony (*Anand karaj*) takes place in the *gurdwara* before midday and involves *lavan* (the recitation of four stanzas from the *Guru Granth Sahib*) in the presence of the bride, the bridegroom and their relatives and friends. The groom comes forward and takes his place in front of the *Guru Granth Sahib*. The bride then joins the congregation and sits at the left side of the groom attended by a sister, sister-in-law or a friend. Whoever is conducting the marriage then asks the couple and their parents to stand whilst he or she prays that God will bless the marriage. The bride and groom publicly assent to the marriage by bowing towards the *Guru Granth Sahib*. When they sit down, the bride's father performs the *palla frowna* ceremony (the bride's father ties the end of his daughter's *dupatta* to the muslin scarf which hangs from the groom's shoulders). The officiator then opens the *Guru Granth Sahib* and the most important ceremony of the marriage is conducted, called *lavan*, the circumlocution around the *Guru Granth Sahib* with the groom leading in each case. The *lavan* (marriage verses) are read and then sung by the *ragis* (religious musicians) as the couple walk slowly round the *Guru Granth Sahib* in a clockwise direction. There are four *lavan*. The service concludes with the singing of the first five and last stanzas of the *Anand* followed by the prayer *Ardas* (Sikh prayer recited at the conclusion of the service) and vak. Finally, the officiating person explains to the couple the duties of married life according to the *Guru's* teachings and makes them aware of their mutual obligations as husband and wife.

The *Anand* marriage is a sacrament and no document is necessary. Here in Britain, there is an arrangement in the *gurdwara* to register the marriage after the wedding according to the law of this country. After the religious ceremony, other celebrations take place at the bride's home, or a hall or hotel. Finally, the marriage party and the bride depart (*doli*) for the groom's home in the late afternoon. The re-marriage of widowers/widows is permitted in Sikhism and the marriage is performed more or less in the same manner. Sikh teachings place an emphasis on family life and as a result few Sikhs remain unmarried. Sikh weddings can take place on any day of the week or in any month of the year. The Sikh teachings suggest that all the days of the week, and all the dates of the month have the same value. Sikh *gurus* ridiculed Astrology and other forms of divination.

1.3 Death

Death is perceived as an ultimate reality in the Sikh tradition and it is the final life cycle rite. When someone dies, relatives and friends are informed and they visit and sit with the family in order to console and support them. The appropriate arrangements are made for the funeral.

According to Sikh traditions, death should not be mourned but accepted as a Will of God. Sikhs believe in *bhana manana* (accepting the Will of God) and see death as part of the natural life circle. They recite *gurbani* and pray for the peace of the departed soul. It is against Sikhism to cry, wail and lament for the departed soul.

"They cry 'alas, alas', and wail for the dead.
They beat their cheeks and pull out their hair.
Did they but cherish the name and practice it.
Nanak, it would be a sacrifice for them.
ਹੈ ਹੈ ਕਰਿ ਕੈ ਓਹਿ ਕਰੇਨਿ ॥ ਗਲਾ ਪਿਟਨਿ ਸਿਰੁ ਖੋਹੇਨਿ ॥
ਨਾਉ ਲੈਨਿ ਅਰੁ ਕਰਨਿ ਸਮਾਇ ॥ ਨਾਨਕ ਤਿਨ ਬਲਿਹਾਰੈ ਜਾਇ ॥ " (GGS: 1410).

Sikhs believe in the doctrine of the transmigration of the soul. According to this, death is regarded as a gradual transition from the human state to another state, depending upon one's conduct (*karma*) in this world. The soul is believed to be immortal although the human body is mortal and has to end.

At death, Sikhs cremate the body. Sikhs believe in cremation though stillborn or little babies are normally buried. In Punjab, the body is cremated on the day of death before sunset, and if someone dies after sunset, that person is cremated as soon as possible the next day. Sikhs living in this country follow the country's funeral arrangements and practices. The cremation ceremony is a family occasion. The deceased is washed and clothed by members of the family, ensuring that the deceased is clothed in the symbols of the faith. The last bath is symbolic of the ritual purification of the body. The body is generally brought home in a coffin before cremation and the family members pray for the soul. The coffin is then taken to the *gurdwara*, where *path* is recited. Other acquaintances and friends see the person for the last time and pray for the deceased's soul. From the *gurdwara*, it proceeds to the crematorium. The sons and brothers of the deceased carry the coffin. At the crematorium, a *granthi* (Sikh priest) leads the mourners in the reading of *Kirtan Sohilla* from the *Guru Granth Sahib*, and this is followed by *Ardas*. Hymns are recited before the cremation. Traditionally, it is the duty of a son to light the pyre. In the absence of a son, one of the male relatives performs this ritual. In the UK, an electric switch is pressed, and some crematoria allow members of the family the privilege of assisting a coffin as it goes into a furnace.

It is normal to return to the *gurdwara* after the funeral for *path bhog* (finishing ceremony of the recitation of the *Granth Sahib*) which is normally sadharan path (a non-continuous recitation of the *Granth Sahib*), kept by the family at their residence or local gurdwara for the peace of the departed soul. Usually the reading of the Holy Book marks the culmination of eleven days of mourning. This is now combined with the funeral in this country. After the *bhog*, there is a turban ceremony if the head of a family has died. On this occasion, relatives bring turban lengths to his successor who is normally the eldest son. The turban tied by him in public is normally brought by his in-laws. The tying of the turban signifies that the responsibility for the family is now his and he has become the head of the family. This is then followed by a communal meal marking the normality of life. It symbolises the continuity of social life and normal activities as opposed to isolation from human contacts, fasting and other ritual manifestations of grief.

Sikhs consign (*parvah*) ashes to running water. The ashes are collected after three days or as soon as possible and these are consigned in a river. The *granthi* accompanies the family on this sad occasion. The erection of memorials and holding a *shradh* (feeding *Brahmans* to honour dead ancestors) is forbidden in Sikhism suggesting if the elders are not cared for in their lifetime then why make offerings in their name after death ਜੀਵਤ ਪਿਤਰ ਨ ਮਾਨੈ ਕੋਉ ਮੂਏਂ ਸਿਰਾਧ ਕਰਾਹੀ ॥ (GGS: 332). The family and the relatives of the deceased will usually make gifts to the poor, to the *gurdwara* or to a charity.

2.0 Sikh religious celebrations

Sikhs have many religious occasions and festivals to celebrate. They celebrate the anniversaries of their *gurus*, called *gurpurabs*. Gurdwaras celebrate *gurpurabs* elaborately, commemorating the births and deaths of the *gurus* and important events in their lives. Some are celebrated more than others. The dates for the Sikh festivals are calculated according to the lunar calendar. A lunar year consists of twelve lunar months based on the time it takes the moon to complete one series of its successive phases, i.e. approximately 29.5 solar days. One full cycle of the lunar phase from full moon to full moon makes a lunar month. On the day of the full moon (*puranmasi*) a month comes to an end, and on the following day (*sangrand*) the next month begins. This indicates that Sikh festivals can not have fixed dates according to the solar (western) calendar for their celebrations. In order to resolve this situation, the *Nanakshahi* (the Sikh calendar named after *Guru* Nanak) calendar was introduced to have fixed dates every year for celebrating anniversaries and festivals. The new calendar makes life much easier for Sikhs as their *gurpurabs* will happen on the same date every year. The calendar does not fix the date for all Sikh festivals. The Sikh festivals that are shared with Hindu traditions such as *Diwali* and *Hola Mohalla* will still have their dates set by the *Vikrami* calendar.

2.1 Sikh *gurpurabs*

Gurdwaras celebrate all *gurpurabs*. Most important are seen to be the birthday of *Guru* Nanak, the martyrdom of *Guru* Arjan Dev, the martyrdom of *Guru* Tegh Bahadur, and the birthday of *Guru* Gobind Singh. All *gurpurab* ceremonies start with *akhand path* (continuous recitation of the entire *Guru Granth Sahib*), which normally begins on Friday morning and finishes on Sunday morning. *Granthis* (readers of the Holy Book) work in relays and the recitation takes approximately forty-eight hours. On the first day of each lunar month (when the sun enters the new Zodiac sign), *sangrand* is celebrated. It is observed with a special service organised in *gurdwaras* and the new month is announced with the reading of the relevant portion, '*Barahmaha*' (hymns relating to twelve months), from the *Guru Granth Sahib*. Many gurdwaras start sadharan path (the ordinary recitation of *Guru Granth Sahib*) on this day and hold *bhog* (the finishing ceremony) on the next *sangrand*. *Langar* is served on all occasions.

2.2 Sikh festivals

Sikhs celebrate many Indian festivals. The Sikh *gurus* gave some of these festivals an added religious interpretation. Among those are *Vaisakhi, Diwali, Hola Mohalla* and *Maghi*. Sikh festivals have both religious and social significance.

Vaisakhi is the most important Sikh festival, named after the second lunar month, *Vaisakh*. It normally falls on the 13th of April. The date is fixed, being based on a solar calendar, though once every thirty six years it occurs on 14th April. It is a summer harvest festival in India and is celebrated by farmers all over the Punjab. *Vaisakhi* may also be interpreted as a festival of renewal; the previous agricultural cycle has come to an end and a new one is about to begin.

Guru Amar Das first institutionalised this as one of the special days when all Sikhs would gather to receive the *Guru's* blessings at Goindwal (Punjab) in 1567. *Guru* Gobind Singh gathered thousands of Sikhs at Anandpur *Sahib* on this day. He created *Khalsa Panth* (order) and gave them a distinctive appearance (ਪਹਿਚਾਣ) on the *Vaisakhi* day in 1699. He also introduced an initiation ceremony. It is compulsory for initiated Sikhs to wear or keep the five symbols known as five 'k's which not only give them a distinct appearance (ਪਹਿਚਾਣ) but also remind them of the pledge to fight against oppression and injustice. Sikhs celebrate *Vaisakhi* as a day of the birth of *Khalsa*.

Vaisakhi is widely celebrated by Sikhs all over the world. Initiation ceremonies are held in *gurdwaras*. *Akhand path* is performed and langar is served for all three days in every *gurdwara* anywhere in the world. *Nagar kirtans*, religious processions, are carried out in many cities of Britain by the Sikh *sangat* (congregation).

Diwali means a festival of lights. It is another festival widely celebrated by Sikhs. It is essentially a Hindu festival and the principal ceremonial observance on the occasion of *Diwali* at the household level is the worship of the images of *Ganesh* and *Lakshmi*, the harbingers of good fortune and prosperity. Hindus commemorate this day as Ramchandra returned to Ayodhya after his fourteen years exile. This is connected with the story of Ramayana, a Hindu epic. The commercial classes clear their old accounts and look to *Diwali* as the beginning of the new business year. This fusion of commercial and religious traditions makes *Diwali* a major social festival. It is also a seasonal festival indicating the onset of the winter season.

Sikhs celebrate this festival because of its religious association with Sikh history. The sixth *guru* of the Sikhs, *Guru* Hargobind was released in 1619 from the Gwalior Fort, where he was imprisoned by the Mughal king Jahangir for nearly two years for not paying the unjust tax called *Jazia* levied on non-Muslims. The *Guru* accepted his release when other fifty-two Rajas (kings) were also released along with him. On this day, he arrived in the city of Amritsar where he was given a tumultuous welcome. On this night, the holy city of Amritsar and Golden Temple was lit to greet the *Guru*. Since then, this tradition is carried on and the lit city of Amritsar is worth seeing on this occasion.

Hola Mohalla is the day after the Spring Equinox. It is essentially a Hindu festival called *Holi*. *Holi* is seasonal in its significance and secular in its celebration. The festival marks the beginning of the Spring season and usually falls in the month of Phagan (February-March) around March 17. There is a Hindu legend attached to this festival called *Prahlad* and *Holika*, signifying the triumph of good over evil. The practice of putting vermillion on the forehead was the original way of celebrating this occasion, which later changed into the sprinkling of dry colours and coloured water on one another. On this day, in 1680, *Guru* Gobind Singh decided to perform mock battles and military exercises in the presence of the Sikh community, stressing the desirability of strength along with the purification of their souls to be able to withstand evil. Since then *Hola* is observed every year by processions displaying weaponry and the importance of social discipline. Anandpur (a city in the Punjab) remains the principal location of this festival. *Gurdwaras* hold diwan (religious programme) and relate the significance of this day.

Maghi falls around 14 January and is named after the Indian lunar month *Magh*. It is connected with the battle of Mukatsar where *Guru* Gobind Singh found forty men from *Majha* (a region of Punjab) who had deserted him during the siege of Anandpur. Their women folk were so ashamed of them that they would not let them enter their homes. The men then returned to reinforce the *Guru's* small army, and died fighting for him. The *Guru* was deeply moved and tore up the paper in front of *Bhai* Maha Singh (one of the *gursikh* fighting the battle) on which they had written their *betaba* (disclaimer) as a sign of forgiveness and reconciliation. He embraced each one of them, as they lay dead or dying and called them the '*Saved Ones*'. This *mela* (festival) of *Maghi* is celebrated in their memory at Mukatsar (Punjab) and many Sikhs go there every year. Sikhs visit *gurdwaras* and listen to *kirtan* on this day to commemorate the martyrdom of the 'Forty Immortals'.

Lohri is a popular seasonal festival which falls on *Makar Sangrand*, around mid January. It is a day for almsgiving and patching up quarrels. A fire is lit and corn, peanuts and sesame sweets are eaten around it. Foods eaten are rice pudding, *halwa*, cornmeal *chapaties* and mustard leaf *saag*. Lohri is celebrated following the birth or a marriage of a son or daughter. This festival is linked to Punjabi cultural traditions rather than religious and as it falls on *sangrand*, it is widely celebrated in the *gurdwaras*.

The celebrations of Sikh ceremonies and festivals have social and religious connotations. It has a special significance in the lives of Sikhs. Sikh ceremonies remind them of Sikh teachings and the requirement of their faith for a purposeful life. The celebrations of *gurpurabs* and festivals are the time for introspection in order to assess that Sikhs are leading their life according to Sikh teachings and principles. The aim of *akhand paths* is to bring them close to the words of their Holy Book by listening, understanding and putting them in practice.

3.0 Summary

Sikhs celebrate many functions and festivals in the *gurdwara*. It is essential for them to conduct their life cycle rites in front of *Guru Granth Sahib* in the presence of family, relatives and congregation. These life cycle rites are birth, naming ceremony (*naamkaran*), wedding (*anand karaj*) and death. For Sikhs a child is a gift from God whether it is a boy or a girl. Every child gets his/her name from the *Granth Sahib*. Marriage is a must for every Sikh as family life is central to the Sikh way of life. Finally death is a natural process in human life and the deceased should not be mourned. Crying and lamenting for the departed soul is against Sikhism. Sikhs should accept the Will of God and remember God's *naam*. Other rituals like fasting, *shradh* (feeding *Brahmans* in the honour of dead) are prohibited in Sikhism.

Sikhs celebrate many *gurpurabs* and festivals. Gurdwaras celebrate all *gurpurabs*. Most important is seen to be the birthday of *Guru* Nanak, the martyrdom of *Guru* Arjan Dev, the martyrdom of *Guru* Tegh Bahadur, and the birthday of *Guru* Gobind Singh. All *gurpurab* ceremonies start with *akhand path* (continuous recitation of the entire *Guru Granth Sahib*), which normally begins on Friday morning and finishes on Sunday morning. On the first day of each lunar month (when the sun enters the new Zodiac sign), *sangrand* is celebrated in *gurdwaras*. It is observed with a special service organised in gurdwaras and the new month is announced. Some festivals celebrated by Sikhs were given added religious interpretation by the *gurus*. *Vaisakhi* is a harvest festival though Sikhs celebrate it as the birthday of the *Khalsa Panth*. *Diwali* is a festival of lights which is celebrated in the memory of greeting the sixth *guru*, Hargobind on his arrival in Amritsar after his release from the Gwalior Fort along with other fifty-two kings. *Diwali* and *Holi* are basically Hindu festivals. *Holi* signifies triumph over evils. The tenth Sikh *guru* stressed the importance of using force to withstand evils when other methods failed. He laid emphasis on the desirability of strength along with the purification of souls to gain victory over evil. On this day of *Hola Mohalla*, in 1680, *Guru* Gobind Singh decided to perform mock battles and military exercises in the presence of the Sikh community. *Maghi* is celebrated in the memory of forty Sikhs who sacrificed their lives for the *Guru* fighting against oppression. *Lohri* is a seasonal festival celebrated for the birth of a child or by a married couple. These two festivals fall on the first day of the lunar month called *sangrand*. Sikhs celebrate all *sangrands* but some are more significant than others.

Chapter 8

Sikh Behaviour and the Sikh Way of Life

1.0 Background

Sikhism is a simple and practical religion. It directs its adherents to lead a moral and pious life while remembering the name of God and submitting to God's Will. There is no need for any rituals according to Sikhism. Sikhism (*Sikhi*) literally means a way of life. Sikh ethics and Sikh religious traditions explain precisely what to believe and how a Sikh should lead his/her life. There is also mention of what to do, called '*rahit*' (ਰਹਿਤ) and what not to do called '*kurahit*' (ਕੁਰਹਿਤ). Sikhs get guidance on the way of life and how they should behave mainly from *Granth Sahib* and the Sikh Code of Conduct. It has a fairly flexible approach and is not a strictly prescriptive religion.

The Sikh Code of Conduct called the Sikh *Rahit Maryada* guides the Sikhs in leading their daily life and to live and work in accordance with the principles of *gurmat*. It is an authorised version on Sikh conduct and customs prepared to achieve uniformity in the religious and social practices of Sikhism. The word *rahit* covers religious and moral life and it includes spiritual and ethical instructions in order to lead a pious life based on the Holy Scripture of Sikhs. Every Sikh is obliged to follow the Sikh Code of Conduct and lead life accordingly. *Guru* Gobind Singh also gave some instructions on how *Khalsa* should live and what they should do (*rahit*) and what not to do (*kurahit*) at the time of the creation of *Khalsa*. The four cardinal sins (*kurahits*) mentioned by him were smoking tobacco and taking other intoxicants; removing and cutting body hairs; eating halal meat (process of slow and ritual killing); adultery and sexual relationship outside marriage. Sikhs should not have any association with narrimar (killing girls at birth). Some of the relevant information is covered in previous chapters such as the concept of God, equality, family life, Sikh ceremonies and festivals. There are some other areas which have not been mentioned in previous chapters and need explaining such as diet, dress, music, relationships, superstitions and other rituals i.e. pilgrimage.

1.1 Diet

The Sikh religion is not prescriptive about diet. As far as food is concerned, it suggests eating what is suited to one's body. One should not eat such food which is harmful for body and mind ਜਿਤੁ ਖਾਧੈ ਤਨੁ ਪੀੜੀਐ ਮਨ ਮਹਿ ਚਲਹਿ ਵਿਕਾਰ ॥ (GGS:

16). Sikhs are both vegetarians and non-vegetarians. Meat is only permitted for consumption if it is *jhatka*, where the animal is killed instantaneously. The *Granth Sahib* contains a number of verses which can be read as rejecting or favouring eating meat. Those who are against eating meat are of the belief that flesh-eating is polluting and should be avoided. Those who opt for it quote "Fools fight over meat. They have no knowledge of the difference between meat and vegetables and which is sin to eat". "ਮਾਸੁ ਮਾਸੁ ਕਰਿ ਮੂਰਖੁ ਝਗੜੇ ਗਿਆਨੁ ਧਿਆਨੁ ਨਹੀ ਜਾਣੈ॥ ਕਉਣੁ ਮਾਸੁ ਕਉਣੁ ਸਾਗੁ ਕਹਾਵੈ ਕਿਸੁ ਮਹਿ ਪਾਪ ਸਮਾਣੇ ॥" (GGS: 1289-1290). Furthermore it is written: 'Man is born from flesh, his *atman* (spirit) lives in flesh. When he is taken from the womb of the flesh he takes a mouthful of milk from teats of flesh'. According to Sikh *Rahit Maryada*, Sikhs should not eat halal meat. Sikh vegetarians see this as the rejection of a particular method of slaughter and not permission to eat meat killed in some other way. However, those who eat meat consider that the prohibition permits the eating of meat killed at a stroke and not bled to death.

Food should be cooked with love and care. Most Sikhs recite *gurbani* while cooking food believing that food cooked with a peaceful mind is healthy. Hands are always washed before touching food. Cleanliness and hygienic processes are strictly observed in the preparation, serving and eating of food.

Sikhs do not eat *jootha* (ਜੂਠਾ) food. There is no equivalent word in English which can give an exact meaning of this concept. The left over food from one's serving is called *jooth*; food eaten or tasted with the used spoon from a dish becomes a *jootha* food. In Sikh homes and *langar*, *jootha* food is not served to anyone.

The Sikh religion forbids the use of any intoxicants or mind-altering substances. Intoxicants, in any shape and form are strictly forbidden except for medicinal purposes. *Gurus* demonstrated a pious life and condemned any food which is harmful for the mind, health and others around including the environment. Therefore, Sikhs are prohibited from consuming tobacco, alcohol or any other intoxicant such as drugs. *Guru* Gobind Singh, the last living *guru* of the Sikhs, listed the use of tobacco as one of the four major acts forbidden to adherents of the Sikh faith.

Hospitality is given great importance in Sikhism and it is a duty of every Sikh to share food with any visitor or hungry person. Sharing food also has religious connotations. Sikh *gurus* placed an emphasis on sharing food and to put this into practice, *langar* (communal food) is served in all *gurdwaras* at the end of a religious service.

Fasting is condemned by the *gurus* as pointless religious observance. It is not sanctioned as a ritual within Sikhism though it is allowed for health reasons. In *Dhanasari Mohalla* 5, it is said:

"Neither worship (of gods), nor fasting, nor a saffron mark, no ablution, nor (customary) charity, contemplating the Lord's Name, one's mind is at peace.
ਪੂਜਾ ਵਰਤ ਤਿਲਕ ਇਸਨਾਨਾ ਪੁੰਨ ਦਾਨ ਬਹੁ ਦੈਨ ॥
ਪ੍ਰਭ ਜੀ ਕੋ ਨਾਮੁ ਜਪਤ ਮਨ ਚੈਨ ॥" (GGS: 674).

1.2 Dress

The Sikh religion does not prescribe any specific dress as long as the body is covered modestly and gracefully. Dress changes from time to time with the advent of new material and fashion. It is suggested to dress in a simple and modest way; gaudy clothes and revealing dress bring no credit. One should not wear anything which causes pain to the body and makes a mind evil ਜਿਤੁ ਪੈਧੈ ਤਨੁ ਪੀੜੀਐ ਮਨ ਮਹਿ ਚਲਹਿ ਵਿਕਾਰ (GGS: 16). Sikh women should not observe the veil (*purdah*) or any other face covering (ਘੁੰਡ). One should not interfere with the body i.e. piercing ears and nose, cutting or dying hair and tattooing.

1.3 Music

Music has been given a special place in Sikh religion. There are three types of music: devotional, folk and classical. Devotional music is particularly favoured by Sikhs as it has tremendous power over the heart and mind of devotees. It frees the mind from a state of sorrow and depression and lends enormous peace. *Gurus* have described music as a means of attaining spiritual joy and transcendental bliss. The Holy Scripture of Sikhs is written in *ragas*. Sikhs have a great musical tradition, beginning with *Guru* Nanak who preached his message accompanied by music. The singing of hymns is called *kirtan*, which literally means singing the praise of God. *Kirtan* is divine music which should bring out clearly the purpose, scope and philosophical content of the hymns set to instrumental music.

Classical music is difficult and complex to understand. It is based on *ragas* and *talas*. The *ragas* divide the octave in hundreds of different ways, each suited to the expression of a particular mood whereas the *tala* reconciles the varying pulses of a thousand different lines through a complex structure of rhythm. *Kirtan* is also performed in classical music. Folk music is generally associated with the social life and is sung on social occasions. Folk songs have enriched Panjabi literature and reflect the social and cultural traditions of the region.

1.4 Other rituals

There were many meaningless rituals and superstitions prevalent in the society as a way to attain God at the beginning of the Sikh religion. These rituals made life hard for ordinary people as it was not always possible to afford them and also these were not helpful to attain spirituality. *Guru* Nanak crusaded against these meaningless traditions and made religion simple to worship. Some of these are given underneath:

1.4.1 Worshipping local shrines and deities

It is against Sikh teachings to visit the shrines of '*pirs*' (saints), *samadhis* (tombs), *jatheras* (cremation sites of village ancestors), '*pitrs*', or ancestor worship and to perform '*shradhs*' (offering food to *Brahmans* for dead elders). '*Shradhs*' fall around October and the belief is that this food will reach the ancestors of those who perform *shradhs*. Sikhs are also forbidden to worship various gods and goddesses. *Brahmans* advised people of suitable days and dates to fix various occasions. Sikhism does not believe in Astrology as all the days of the week and months of the years are the same for Sikhs.

1.4.2 Pilgrimage

Pilgrimage is disapproved of in the Sikh religion and the gurus frequently referred to this custom as a wasted effort:

"Why should I go to bathe at the pilgrim-places?
Naam is the only sacred place of pilgrimage.
The Holiest of the Holy baths is the contemplation of the Word
that gives inner light and spiritual illumination
ਤੀਰਥਿ ਨਾਵਣ ਜਾਉ ਤੀਰਥੁ ਨਾਮੁ ਹੈ ॥ ਤੀਰਥੁ ਸਬਦ ਬੀਚਾਰੁ ਅੰਤਰਿ ਗਿਆਨੁ ਹੈ ॥ " (GGS: 687)

Sikh *gurus* gave no importance to pilgrimage and did not suggest any moral or spiritual gain from it. But there are many sacred and historic places in India and Pakistan associated with important events in the lives of the *gurus* which are revered by Sikhs. Many Sikhs visit (ਯਾਤਰਾ-*yatra*) these places out of respect and not for religious obligation. It is important to mention some of the very special *gurdwaras* every Sikh wants to visit. *Gurdwara Janamsthan*, the birthplace of *Guru* Nanak is in Nankana *Sahib* (Pakistan). It was built with the

approval of *Maharaja* Ranjit Singh in 1819-1820. *Harmandar Sahib* is the most sacred shrine for Sikhs, built by the fifth *guru* and the foundation stone was laid by a Muslim saint *Mian* Mir in 1588. *Maharaja* Ranjit Singh donated a large amount of gold for the dome and roof in 1803 and since then has been known as the Golden Temple.

Gurdwara Sis Ganj is situated on the site where the ninth guru Tegh Bahadur  gave his life for the freedom of speech and worship; gurdwara Bangla Sahib where the eighth guru Harkrishan stayed are well known shrines in Delhi. Hemkunt (lake of ice) Sahib is another Sikh shrine increasingly visited by devout Sikhs. It is situated in the Himalayas at about 15,210 feet above sea level in the Chamoli district of Uttar Pradesh (Uttranchal). The gurdwara was built in 1936 and it stands on the bank of the lake in a narrow valley surrounded by high mountains capped by seven peaks. It is the place of meditation and prayer of the tenth guru where it is believed, he achieved union with God. The temple commemorates the Guru's mission to teach the true religion and rid people of evil ways.

The five Sikh takhts (seats of authority) are also worth mentioning. The Akal takht situated directly opposite Harmandar Sahib was built by the sixth guru Hargobind in 1609. It is the highest seat of authority for Sikhs all over the world and any laws to do with Sikhism are issued from here. The second takht Sri Patna Sahib in Bihar was built to commemorate the birth of the tenth guru Gobind Singh. The third takht Sri Keshgarh Sahib in Anandpur (Punjab) is the place where the tenth guru created the Khalsa. The fourth takht Sri Dam Dama Sahib in Punjab is a place where Guru Gobind Singh rested for a year and in 1706, he revised the Adi Granth at this place. This place is also well known for Dam Damai Taksal (religious school) known for authentic Sikh literature. The fifth takht Sri Hazur Sahib in Maharastra is a place known for converting a monk Banda Bahadur into a soldier and general. It is also a place where the tenth guru renamed Adi granth to be Guru Granth Sahib. Guru Gobind Singh also died here. Many devout Sikhs visit these historical places and other gurdwaras but Sikhs have no compulsion that they must visit these sites in their life time.

2.0 Sikh greetings

Sat Sri Akal (ਸਤਿ ਸ੍ਰੀ ਅਕਾਲ) is a Sikh greeting which is obligatory for every Sikh. When Sikhs meet, they say *Sat Sri Akal* meaning *sat* (truth), *sri* (great) and *Akal* (timeless being i.e. God). It makes 'Truth is God'. The complete usage is *jo bole so nihal, Sat Sri Akal* (ਜੋ ਬੋਲੈ ਸੋ ਨਿਹਾਲ ਸਤਿ ਸ੍ਰੀ ਅਕਾਲ) meaning one who says God is truth is blessed. When two Sikhs meet, they always greet each other with these words with folded hands near the chest, head slightly bowed in a humbling and respectful posture, bending forward and downwards keeping the legs straight indicating submission and respect for the Almighty God. The greeting is both spoken and shown by body gesture.

There is another form of Sikh greetings mainly used by the *amritdhari* Sikhs *Vaheguru ji ka Khalsa Vaheguru ji ki fateh* meaning the *Khalsa* belongs to God and victory belongs to God. Both the greetings are said with folded hands and bent body just to show respect for each other. It is related to remembering the name of God.

3.0 Summary

Sikh behaviour and way of life is guided by *Granth Sahib* and the Sikh Code of Conduct. Some of the related information has already been given in previous chapters such as basic beliefs, attitude towards humanity and environment, equality, family life and life cycle rites. This chapter provides information on Sikh diet, dress, music, stand on meaningless rituals; pilgrimage and the historic *gurdwaras* and *takhts* visited by Sikhs and finally Sikh greetings. Sikhs should eat what is suitable to their bodies. This covers what to eat and what to avoid, hospitality, food hygiene and fasting. Dress for Sikhs should be modest and women should not cover their faces. Piercing and tattooing is not allowed. No body hair should be removed. Music has a special place in Sikh religion as the Sikh Holy Book is written in *ragas* and the hymns are sung in *kirtan*. Sikhs are strictly prohibited from performing unnecessary rituals. There is no place for superstitions, idol worship and astrology in Sikhism.

Chapter 9

Roots and Routes: An Interfaith Dialogue

I am a Christian and a Methodist Minister and my roots are in Sikhism. I was born into a deeply religious Sikh family. I was brought up in an area of Nairobi, Kenya where people of such various backgrounds as Hinduism, Sikhism, Islam, and people of African traditional religions lived side by side. Members of my family have such depths of the awareness of God and relationship with God, and such a depth of spirituality, that in Kenya our house was never far away from the *gurdwara* and we never moved more than a quarter of a mile away from the *gurdwara* Members of my own family shared in the leading of worship. My grandfather shared in the reading of Scriptures in worship, and so did my mother. I spent hours in the *gurdwara* for worship, worship that is centred on the word of God, and where the mixture of reading of scriptures and the smell of incense combines in such a way that when you are there the very atmosphere is like the breath of God. I enjoyed stories from the life of *Guru* Nanak Dev. He taught that all people are made from the same clay; he believed God is present everywhere; he taught people to meditate on the Name of God and to serve the poor; he valued honestly earned bread as opposed to riches gained through exploitation. At the centre of the Sikh faith and community is worship and food. Every visit to a *gurdwara* includes being served food in *Langar*. *Guru* Amar Das gave the formula: *Pahile Pangat Phir Sangat*, "First we eat, then we meet". With eating, of course, goes serving. It is a joy to be a host, and to offer *seva* (service), to serve the food, to wash up. The *gurdwara* compound was my playground as a young boy. I attended the Sikh Boys and Girls School where I learned Panjabi and studied the Sikh scriptures. In this Sikh context, my own experience of God developed into a deep relationship of love and of trust. Within Sikhism I understood God as Father and Mother, Friend and Companion. To quote an often repeated verse: "You are my Mother, you are my Father."

The faith and scriptures that fired and fed my emotions and spirituality in my younger life came from the Sikh community, and my Sikh family. When Kenya became an independent country (1963/1964), my parents chose to bring the family to UK and I started attending a local Church in Dudley, West Midlands.

1.0 Jesus Christ: In Communion with the excluded

I began to read the New Testament and encountered Jesus Christ and his teachings. I was captivated by Jesus' compassion for the poor in particular. I was impressed by his respect for different faiths, an aspect of Jesus' ministry that is inadequately articulated in Churches. He pointed to the compassion with which a Samaritan treated someone in need and urged others to "do likewise"; he pointed to a Roman leader, and to a Canaanite Woman and commented on their "great faith". Perhaps Jesus' most radical and subversive and challenging activity, for which he was ridiculed, was to eat with the poorest, and to include the excluded in his company. He kept an Open Table, a Table for all.

What I find compelling in Jesus is this:

- Jesus expresses God who is with us all;

- Jesus gives priority to people who are poor, and gives respect to people of other faiths;

- Jesus eats with those people that others exclude;

- Jesus dies abandoned by friends;

- Jesus' living and loving has inspired countless billions of people.

Jesus Christ pointed to the inclusiveness of the Kingdom of God. He broke barriers and included those that others excluded, socially and spiritually. He welcomed the poor, "the unclean" and "the sinners" and ate with them. He respected people of other faiths, cultures and nations. This is a part of his story that is not always articulated. He turned over the tables which exploited people financially and spiritually, and which excluded people to such an extent that even their prayers were not valued. "My house," he declared in God's name, "shall be called a house of prayer for all nations" (Mark 11:17). And, because of this, he risked his life, and was executed.

The one who stands by those that others reject is rejected; the one who befriends the poor is denied by his best friends; the one who respects others is mocked and ridiculed by opponents; the one who desires life abundant for others is denied life and dies a cruel death; the one who speaks truth and seeks justice is executed as a blasphemer and criminal. The one in whom we see God who is with us cries out: "my God, my God, why have you forsaken me?" (Mark 15:34).

This is the point at which Jesus' story touched me. This is the unique feature about Jesus for me in a world of many faiths and many messengers of God. Jesus identifies with those who are excluded and suffer, to the point of being broken and death. In this Jesus shows God's way, God's truth and God's life. Jesus illustrates a holiness of connectedness not separateness, of intimacy not aloofness. His example and teachings disclose clues and ways to live and to interpret life.

Indian *Dalit* theology describes Jesus as the one who identifies with the *Dalits*, the self designation by people who suffer through exclusion by society. The term *Dalit* comes from *"Dal"* which means crushed, broken. It is the name given to broken, split red lentils, for example. It is one of the cheapest forms of food and feeds the poorest. Jesus is *Dalit*. Jesus connects through food, and shows us how to engage with the most marginalised people. Jesus did not feel he was polluted, made impure, in any way through contact with people considered by others to be "the lowliest, lowest and the least".

The genius of Jesus was to put food, a meal, at the centre of his community. He said "whenever you meet in my name, have a meal and remember me" (Luke 22:19).

So often Churches present Jesus as a dull man and make following Jesus a tedious and serious business. Food should be at the heart of worship and life. The Holy Communion should sum up what Churches represent. It should be placed in the context of the many meals Jesus shared with others, especially the poorest. The Holy Communion should nurture in us lifestyles that will end hunger, greed and inequality, the biggest scandals of the world's community.

I want to move on now to say something about my understanding of God from a Christian perspective.

2.0 God: Immense, unfathomed, and unconfined

Jesus taught his disciples a prayer. It is commonly referred to as "the Lord's Prayer". The Prayer reads: "Our Father in heaven, hallowed be your name. Your Kingdom come, your will be done, on earth as it is in heaven. Give us this day our daily bread. Forgive us our sins as we forgive them that sin against us. Lead us not into temptation, but deliver us from evil." (Matthew 6:9-13)

When we pray "Our Father in heaven, hallowed be your Name" we acknowledge a close relationship with God, but we are not at the same time confining God to "our" own circle of faith and community. To locate God in heaven is not to place a boundary around God's presence and realm of activity. It is certainly not to say that God is far and remote from us, "up there" or "out there". To refer to God as Father is not to confine God to a particular gender or to characterise God as some of the violent, abusive or absent Father figures we may be aware of or hear about in news stories. While Christians want to say that God is like Jesus Christ, who is seen as a physical expression of what God is like, it would be a very restricted understanding of God to say that this sums up what God is like completely.

To say "Our Father in heaven" is to acknowledge that God, and God's Grace is without boundaries. The presence and work of God is not restricted to just one faith. God is not without witness anywhere in the world. God is neither confined to, nor defined by, any one religious tradition. Because God's presence is not confined to any one religion or geographical area, it is essential for people of different faiths to acknowledge, in all honesty and humility, that no one faith has a monopoly of the truth about God. What is needed is for people of different faiths to meet with each other, share experiences of God, and grow in our understanding of God and of each other.

God is One, the Father/Mother of us all. God desires "the fullness of life" (John 10:10) for each human being.

3.0 Image of God: Equality

The Christian faith affirms that all human beings are made in the Image of God (Genesis 1:26-27).

To say we are all made in the Image of God is to acknowledge that all human beings are members of one race, the human race; that in the eyes of God our status is not determined by where we were born, what religion we profess, what gender or skin colour we are, or by our abilities, disabilities, sexual orientation or age; that God's breath or grace is in each person and life is sacred and of worth, and should be treated with respect. Another way of putting this is to say that all people are the children of God, and that no one should be treated as anything less. Each human being is unique. This means that human diversity is part of God's will and purpose.

4.0 Body of Christ: Diversity

There is a passage in the New Testament (1 Corinthians 12: 12-27) which depicts members of the Church as members of a human body. Members of the Church are seen as different parts of the body. Just as all parts of the body – arms, eyes, ears, nose, feet are important – so are all members of the Church.

A foot cannot say to a hand, "you do not belong to the body", and so on. Each part is important and has a place in the body. In the same way, all members of the Church community are equally important, none can be despised. One member can not say to another, "you don't belong here". The New Testament passage sees the Church members as members of the Body of Christ.

The Body of Christ imagery specifically addresses the Christian community, recognising each member as essential and integral to the whole. The understanding of the Body of Christ, of course, is not complete without recognition of the brokenness and scars of the Body of Christ. If we do not take account of the broken Body of Christ in his suffering and crucifixion, we run the danger of excluding the experience of hurting, abused, exploited, "disabled", members.

God without boundaries, the inclusiveness of Jesus Christ, the Image of God, and the Body of Christ... these are powerful tools and theologies Christians have and offer to deepen our calling to build inclusive communities, congregations and Churches.

These theologies allow no place for racism, sexism, homophobia, religious bigotry or any kind of discrimination in Christian theology and practice. They are at the heart of Christian reflections and debates regarding equalities and diversity in our practice. They require that we take extraordinary care to embed equality and diversity in all our thinking and practice and interfaith dialogue. Our practice in every sphere of our lives should be committed to challenging and eradicating discrimination not least in employment, education, economic improvement and ecumenism.

There is also an acknowledgement here that the Christian faith and Church is centred on the Body of Christ, not bricks and mortar. The Church is the congregation, not the building. Buildings have their value, many are centres of pilgrimage. Jesus spoke of the Temple of his Body (John 2:21). There is an understanding in the Christian faith that God lives within us. Our human body is the Temple of God and should be honoured as such. It is within ourselves and in our relationships with others that we have the deepest experiences of God. We need to take responsibility for our selves, our health, our bodies - each one of us is sacred - made in the image of God, and our body is the Temple of God.

5.0 Christianity: A way of life

Jesus' primary message related to what he called "the Kingdom of God". This is an environment and a realm where God rules. Jesus told stories (parables) to describe the Kingdom of God. At the very least in the Kingdom of God the poorest are given priority and poverty is brought to an end, oppression is eliminated, debt is cancelled, hunger is an unacceptable offence, relationships are characterised by forgiveness and respect, and people facing trials and tribulations of any kind are given support.

A minimal expression of this way of life is summed up in the words: Love God, and love your neighbour as yourself.

In one of his parables Jesus places right behaviour above right belief, and said that faith is judged by how you treat those in greatest need. In fact it is in seeing and serving those in greatest need that one sees and serves Christ. His words of welcome and affirmation in the Kingdom of God are addressed to those of whom he can say: "I was hungry and you fed me, thirsty and you gave me a drink; I was a stranger and you welcomed me in your homes, naked and you clothed me; I was sick and you took care of me, in prison and you visited me" (Matthew 25:35-36).

The Bible insists that God's relationship with human beings is defined by God's amazing and endless grace.

6.0 The Bible: Sacrament of Grace

The Bible is a library of books in one cover and has two sections. Section one contains Hebrew Scriptures sacred to Jews and also to Christians, and often referred to as the Old Testament. Section two, referred to as the New Testament, and is centred on the story and teachings of Jesus Christ and his earliest followers. The books of the Bible record reflections and stories of peoples' experiences of God and include poetry, prose, psalms, parables, history, narrative, sermons, prayers, songs, and dreams and visions. These are considered holy and sacred by Christians who discern in them the word and ways of God, and what God is like. The Bible has been described as a Sacrament that discloses God and the word of God, but is not worshipped as God. Reading the Bible and meditating on its words is food and nourishment for the soul. The Bible has central place in Christian worship. There is considerable theological reflection on Biblical words, stories and texts.

7.0 Grace: The *Adi Granth* and New Testament

Grace is one of the great words of Christian and Sikh Scriptures. In the *Adi Granth* of the Sikhs the word *Prashad*, translated as Grace occurs over 600 times. Add to this the words *Kirpa* and *Nadir* also translated as Grace, and we find that the term Grace is found on practically every page of the Scriptures that are Sacred to Sikhs. Likewise, in the New Testament the word Grace, or the manifestation of Grace is on practically every page. The concept of Grace in Sikhism is complex but, ultimately, it refers to God who is with people and to

God's attention and gaze being fixed upon people. In Sikhism Grace is mediated through the *Guru*. The *Mool Mantra* concludes with *Gurprashad* (literally, "grace through the *Guru*").

Biblically, Grace is the description of God's abundant gifts and generosity. In the New Testament, Grace is related to Jesus Christ:

> "Grace and Truth came through Jesus Christ" (John 1:17).
> "From his fullness we have received grace upon grace" (John 1:16).

The New Testament insists that life in the Kingdom of God is a gift of the Grace of God. This is well stated in the words:

> "By Grace you have been saved through faith, and this is not your own doing; it is the gift of God – not the result of works, so that no one may boast" (Eph 2:8-9).

Grace is the gift and generosity of God given in Jesus Christ. This refers especially to the gifts of mercy and forgiveness.

As in the New Testament, so in Sikh writings also, salvation is the work of Grace, a gift of God. Sikhs pray daily using these words of the *Japji Sahib*:

> "Good actions may procure a better frame of life, but salvation comes only through His Grace" (Japji 2)

8.0 Prayer: Listening to God

Prayer is an integral part of Christian spirituality, at personal and congregational level. Because God is with us, all can pray. It is not only the work of leaders of worship. Our approach to prayer is influenced by our understanding of where God is, the ways of God and the Grace of God. There is also a connection between prayer and our understanding of suffering and the causes of suffering. Is God with us always, or is God called into situations by prayer and petition? Can God be persuaded to act in particular ways by human prayer? Is suffering caused by God, is it the result of bad (sinful) behaviour? So what are we doing when we pray?

Prayer is not about what we say and the length of the time we spend saying it. The Prayer Jesus taught his Disciples (quoted above) is remarkably short. In my view prayer is certainly not about telling God how to order the world and what to do, or to ask God to intervene in particular situations. Prayer is an approach to the whole of life. It is about listening to God, and discerning what God is calling us to do, and then responding with appropriate action. There is value also in holding, or remembering people or places, or situations, before God – not because God does not already know. It is good to share with someone else what matters to us. Prayer does include sharing with God exactly how you feel, including expressions of disbelief at what is happening, and outrage or anger at what you or others may be going through. Even Jesus cried out, "My God, my God, why have you forsaken me?" (Mark 15:34)

There are numerous approaches to prayerful listening. It is possible to read a passage of Scripture and quietly reflect on it. This can be done privately or with others. Sometimes it is good to simply spend some time in silence. Silence can aid listening. Silence is not the absence of noise, but a capacity to shut up, pay attention, and listen deeply, with a still mind. In the listening there can be a moment of revelation and discovery. Such silence can be achieved in the midst of noise as well as in a quiet atmosphere. Prayer is also about deeper levels of listening, connection and communication between human beings and God. What particularly distinguishes holy and spiritual leaders from the rest of us is that they learned to listen, connect and communicate at these deeper levels. Perhaps this is the connection between prayer and healing. We are not all profound spiritual leaders, but we can all pray. The One God of all hears the prayers of all people of all faiths, and of people who profess no particular religious faith.

9.0 Uniqueness: Only one way to God?

There are Christians who insist that apart from Christ there is no knowledge of God and no salvation, and quote words attributed to Jesus: "No one comes to the Father but by me; I am the way, the truth and the life" (John 14:6)). Others are equally clear that God is not the prisoner of the Christian faith or community, and is active in all faiths, in all of life and love, healing, feeding and challenging, and shares the pain of human distress.

9.1 Is Jesus the only way to God?

People of many faiths other than Christian claim deep experience of God, and address God as Father and Mother. How can we know that there is experience of God apart from having a relationship with Jesus Christ? I believe that in our multi-faith world we all need to engage in conversation with people of different faiths about this subject.

9.2 Conversation is a good method for theological reflection.

I take every opportunity I get to be in conversation with people of different faiths about the words of John 14:6. The most remarkable conversation I have held was with the Supreme Sikh leader *Jathedar* Mohinder Singh, in Amritsar

(February 2001), when I was president of the Methodist Conference. I had with me thirty other Methodists, and we met the *Jathedar* in *Akal Takht* in the grounds of Harmandar Sahib, the Golden Temple. The Bishop of Amritsar Rt Rev Somantaroy was there too as were representatives of the Press. Journalists kept trying to divert the conversation to their own question: "What do you think about this man, he left the Sikh faith and converted to Christianity and now comes here as president of the Methodist Church?" The *Jathedar* completely ignored their questions and focussed on his conversation with me. I had one big question for him. "*Jathedar Ji*, there is a verse in the Bible which suggests that no one can come to God or have experience of God except through Jesus Christ. What is your response to that?"

The *Jathedar* did not ridicule the Bible. He simply stated, "God is with us all and is everywhere. Just as surely as there is cream in milk, though we cannot see the cream, so God is in the world and in us, though we cannot see God." Though he did not put it in these words, the *Jathedar* was saying that God is with us all, and God is in this place and all places. He was also saying that many people experience God without a relationship with Jesus Christ.

Sikh Theology insists that God is with us, and is our *Mata* (Mother) and *Pita* (Father). Sikh Theology rejects the idea that God can take flesh and be born as a human being. The central text in Sikhism, the *Mool Mantra*, contains an important word: *Ajuni* (without birth and death). God does not take birth and is outside the circle of birth and death. God is manifest and made known not as a human being but as Truth (*Sat*), as Name (*Nam*), as Word (*Shabad*). These are Sikh concepts of revelation, and in these ways God is continually being disclosed and encountered.

Sikh-Christian dialogue would be enriched by a search for a deeper understanding of the concepts of Word and *Shabad*, Name and *Nam*, Grace, Incarnation and *Ajuni*.

10.0 Only one way: God comes to us and is with us

The good news disclosed and proclaimed in Jesus Christ, and celebrated in Christianity is that God is with us, and comes to us, always. This is what Christians celebrate at Christmas. This is also the message of Easter, that even death cannot remove us from the presence of God. There is indeed "only one way" disclosed in Jesus. There is only God's way to us.

I personally do not believe different religions are different pathways to God. I do not like the analogy of the mountain with different pathways to the top, seeing all religions as different pathways to God. We don't go to God. We don't have to look or search for God. God comes to us. God is with us.

For me loyalty and commitment to Jesus goes hand in hand with openness to people of other faiths and the searching challenges they present to Christians. It is essential for people of different faiths to meet and share our faith stories and experiences of God with each other. As we do so we will all grow in our understanding of God, and God's will and work and ways. This is part of the process to build relationships of deep respect between people of different faiths. Within relationships of respect, Christians will share the good news of God disclosed in Jesus Christ without arrogance, and as appealingly and attractively as possible.

11.0 Ethical test: Theological reflection that works

There is a strong tradition of theological reflection in Christian history. There is a recognised discipline of academic theology, and there is also a practical theology. At the simplest level, the former engages critically with the work of scholars and the latter is a critical reflection of the experience of God in daily life. Most Church members would not think of themselves as theologians in the former style.

Theology is literally words about God (theos: God; logos: word). In that sense we are all theologians. We constantly hold conversations in which we share words about God. We are all made in the Image of God. Our bodies are the Temple and dwelling place of God. We all have our own unique experiences and stories of God to share.

A question worth asking about any theological reflection is: Does it work? "By their fruit you shall know them" said Jesus in relation to his disciples. This test can be applied to behaviour and to theology. According to this test, any theology that leads to or justifies behaviour that is judged to be unethical would itself be unethical, and would need to be re-examined; question marks are raised against behaviour and attitudes that are destructive and harmful towards people who are different, people of "other faiths", other ethnicities or skin colours. Destructive and oppressive theology is ethically unacceptable. On the other hand, a positive, ethically acceptable theology is one that makes a constructive contribution to human and environmental well being. Creative, edifying and life giving theology is ethically acceptable. Dr Rait's work certainly falls in the latter category, and I am glad to share in it.

What I offer in my chapter is not an academic theological paper. 'Roots and Routes' is my own theological reflections arising out of my own experience of God within my Sikh roots and Christian experience.

Chapter 10

Conclusion

The Sikh religion is a practical religion with a modern approach. It is ranked as the world's fifth largest religion followed by just over twenty three million people. Sikhism is a way of life which can be followed by anyone irrespective of their gender, caste, class, colour and creed. Its teachings contain a message of truth for the whole of humanity and not that of any specific group or community. It is regarded as a distinct faith bringing radical changes to the existing society suffering from inequality and fanaticism.

A Sikh is a disciple of ten *gurus* and believes and practices the teachings of *Guru Granth Sahib*, the Holy Scripture of the Sikhs. Sikhism is based on reciting the name of God, submitting to God's Will, earning an honest living (emphasis on work ethos and not being a burden on anyone) and sharing with the poor and needy. The core values are equality, voluntary service and leading a family life. It gives importance to noble deeds and rejects the caste system. It promotes gender and social equality and recommends voluntary service to the wider community. Sikhism teaches truthful living free from superstitions and meaningless rituals. Sikhs are easily recognised by their distinct appearance. Their behaviour and way of life is guided by *Granth Sahib* and the Sikh Code of Conduct.

Guru Nanak was the founder of the Sikh religion. He was succeeded by nine successor *gurus* who preached the message of Sikhism. *Gurus* in Sikhism are mere guides and teachers. Their teachings were recorded in the *Guru Granth Sahib*. It was first compiled in 1604 by the fifth guru Arjan Dev and *Guru* Gobind Singh, the tenth and last living *guru* of the Sikhs added the hymns of his father and possibly one couplet of his own in 1705. He bestowed it with the *Guruship* in 1708, putting an end to the tradition of *Guruship* in an individual person. The *Granth Sahib* is considered to be the living embodiment of *Gurus* and the ultimate *Guru* of Sikhs called '*Word Guru*'. It also includes the compositions of saints and mystics of other religions and regions, who expressed the common concepts such as absurdity of religious rituals, the hatred of idolatry, castelessness and gender equality. The uniqueness of this Scripture is that it was written by the *gurus* and put together during the life time of its compilers and whose authenticity has never been questioned. It is written in *ragas* and Sikhism gives great importance to music as it is soothing to the ears and nourishing for the mind. *Gurus* employed homely and simple metaphors and used the language understood by lay persons to make their message easily accessible to the ordinary people. *Guru Granth Sahib* is written in Panjabi using *Gurmukhi* script though the largest portion of the *Granth* was composed in Hindvi, a mixture of western Hindi, Prakrit, Brij and Panjabi. There is also the use of Sanskrit, Arabic and Persian words. So, not only in subject matters, or religious affiliations of its authors, but also in language, the *Granth* upholds the synthesis of creeds as against exclusiveness of form. It is a great original source of the socio-cultural history of the medieval period particularly of North India. *Guru Granth Sahib* teaches about God and creation, and about humans and their place in the universe and how a person can seek enlightenment and salvation. It preaches love for human beings and God's creation. It gives the message of love, harmony, human dignity, and service towards humanity, caring for God's creation, remembering God and doing good deeds in order to liberate the soul aiming for an ultimate unity with God. This *Granth* is not only meant for Sikhs but also for all people who believe in the existence of God and love for humanity and God's creation. Sikhism respects all other religions and does not consider any religion superior or inferior. Religions evolve and develop their modes of worship and religious traditions within the context of their social environment.

The central teaching in Sikhism is the belief in the concept of the oneness of God and lays emphasis on the unity of God being creator, sustainer and destroyer. God is a supreme power, whose extent is unknown. According to Sikhism, God existed all alone in the state of contemplation and there was darkness and chaos for millions of years. This universe is the creation of God and there are many more constellations. Everything created by God has its own place in this planet and exists for a reason and purpose. God resides within human beings and remains present in every element of God's own creation. God created humans as superior and put a divine spark and immortal soul in their bodies. It is their duty to be devoted and loyal to their creator and have respect for God's creation. Nature and human life is interdependent for their existence and survival. Because of the coexistence nature, humans should know their own boundaries and should not interfere in God's layout and creation. They should learn to live in harmony with and not to confront nature. It is necessary to preserve this relationship for the healthy existence of this planet. It is evident that intrusion by humans and scientists through modern technology into nature's territory has resulted in enormous damage to the environment and ecology bringing unpredictable changes in climate and weather. Climate change is undeniably real and obviously caused by human activities. The importance of human relations with nature has become more evident in the face of global challenge impacting environment. The Sikh religion protects the environment and ecology and the *gurus* suggested practical ways to preserve natural resources.

Sikhism was a progressive religion well ahead of its time when it was founded in the 15th Century. The very basis of Sikhism is its belief in human equality which is shown in the words and practices of the *gurus*. There is no basis for discrimination in the Sikh faith in regard to caste, race, gender, religion or socioeconomic standing. No one is superior or inferior but the actions of people determine their place in society. The compositions of the *Guru Granth Sahib* exhibit this non-discriminatory policy by including the hymns of saints of other religions and lower classes. The Sikh religion also promotes a classless society, giving more importance to virtue than wealth suggesting that the spiritual realisation can be attained by anyone with noble deeds. Discrimination on the basis of caste is also severely criticised by Sikh *gurus*.

The practical initiatives taken by the Sikh *gurus* are indicative of their strong belief in equality. *Gurus* introduced certain traditions to eradicate discrimination such as *langar*. It is representative of an acknowledgment of social equality and integration. In this practice, any person regardless of caste, class or social status eats together sitting side by side in a row (*pangat*). This is a unique tradition introduced by the Sikh *gurus* which is still thriving and *langar* is served in all the *gurdwaras* anywhere in the world. The tenth *guru* demonstrated further the principle of equality through the initiation ceremony. He created *Khalsa Panth* by bringing people from different occupations and backgrounds and declared caste to be a hindrance to the unity of the *Khalsa* (pure ones).

Sikhism advocates gender equality and accords women an equal place in society. The Sikh *gurus* adopted a two-fold approach to gender issues. They took a positive attitude towards women in order to enhance their status and prestige. *Gurus* raised their voice not to treat women as subservient to men and mere perpetuators of the race. Demeaning women was discouraged by *gurus* suggesting they play a dominant role in preparing the future generations. They opposed the social traditions undermining women and those were discarded such as veiling of women, sati and female infanticide. They were encouraged to participate in all walks of life including religious performances. Sikh *gurus* tried to revolutionise the society which treated women and the social outcast worse than animals.

Family life is central to the Sikh way of life. Renunciation is condemned and Sikhs are encouraged to lead a family life unattached to gross materialism. The emphasis is given to the institution of marriage. It is important for every Sikh to marry including Sikh priests. Divorcees, widows or widowers are allowed to remarry. The Sikh marriage is known as *Anand karaj* (*Anand* means bliss and *karaj* means ceremony). Marriage according to Sikhism is a sacrament and not a civil contract. It takes place in front of *Guru Granth Sahib* binding a couple in a permanent relationship. Marriage should be simple and compatible. Elaborate and lavish marriage arrangements and the giving of a dowry are not the Sikh ways of life. In the family there should be love and harmony in the relationship of a husband and wife. Elderly parents should be respected and cared for and the children should be given a good upbringing based on Sikhism. Marriage across caste is permitted since caste system is condemned in the Sikh religion. Child marriage is prohibited so is adultery and polygamy. Family planning, use of contraceptives, homosexuality and marriage with lesbians and gays are not referred to in the Sikh Scripture as it may not have been an issue at the time of their writing. It is a sin to destroy life and hence deliberate miscarriage or abortion is not approved of. Similarly, experimenting with embryos and foetus aborting is discouraged. Aborting a foetus is a modern form of female infanticide. Mercy killing is also disapproved of by Sikhism on the basis that suffering and pain are the result of one's actions and deeds. Taking life in one's own hands or killing or aborting is defying the Will of God.

Sikhs celebrate many functions and festivals. The Sikh ceremonies for birth, marriage and death have special significance in Sikh religion. These life cycle rites help them to maintain an identity, a high degree of cohesiveness and link them to the faith traditions. Every child gets his/her name from the Holy Book; marriage takes place in front of the *Guru Granth Sahib* and finally the last journey of death departs from the *gurdwara*. For Sikhs a child is a gift from God whether it is a boy or a girl. Both should be treated the same. Death is considered to be a natural process in human life. The deceased should not be mourned. Crying and lamenting for the departed soul is against Sikhism. Sikhs should submit to God's Will and pray for the departed soul. Fasting and *shradh* are prohibited in Sikhism.

The celebrations of *gurpurabs* are the time of reflection and introspection for Sikhs. *Gurdwaras* celebrate all *gurpurabs*. Most important is seen to be the birthday of *Guru* Nanak and *Guru* Gobind Singh; the martyrdom of *Guru* Arjan Dev and of *Guru* Tegh Bahadur. All *gurpurab* ceremonies start with akhand path which normally begins on Friday morning and finishes on Sunday morning. The first day of each lunar month *sangrand* is celebrated in *gurdwaras*. The teachings of the *gurus* are reinforced on these occasions. *Vaisakhi* is significant for initiation ceremonies and for Sikhs, taking *amrit* is an expression of total commitment towards the Sikh faith. Initiation is seen as the way to spiritual development when coupled with adherence to the ethical principles of Sikhism. The ceremony is for women as well as for men and takes place at an age when the person can understand its significance. *Khalsa*

Panth was created on this day in 1699 and it is the reminder of equality, Sikh identity and a prescribed way of life *(rahit)*. *Hola Mohalla* stressed the importance of using force to withstand evils when other methods failed. *Guru* Gobind Singh laid emphasis on the desirability of strength along with the purification of souls to gain victory over evil. *Diwali* is essentially a Hindu festival also celebrated by Sikhs. It marks new beginnings and a renewal of commitment to family values, whilst representing joy, resolution and forgiveness. The spiritual meaning of *Diwali* is the realisation of the inner light 'soul' as the guide for truthful living which outshines all darkness and dispels all ignorance. It brings the message of freedom and justice. The lifecycle rites and festivals are bound by religion and religious traditions. Sikhs should celebrate them by reciting *bani* and keeping the Sikh values in mind. It is a reminder for Sikhs to assess and compare their attitude to the Sikh way of life.

Sikhism believes in a simple way of life guided by the Holy Book and the Sikh Code of Conduct. The Sikh *gurus* made *seva* (voluntary service) a prerequisite to spiritual development. Sikh *gurus* repeatedly emphasised that *haumen* (individualism or self-centredness) is at the root of the problems from which the individual and society suffer. One should free oneself from the evil manifestations of *haumen*, i.e. lust, anger, greed, attachment and pride and replace them with five virtuous qualities: self-control, forgiveness, contentment, love for God and humility. The Sikh diet should be simple and nourishing for body and mind. Food should be cooked with love and care. Those who eat meat should eat *jhatka*. Sikhs are advised to abstain from *halal* (meat slaughtered by the process of slow and ritual killing). Fasting as a ritual is condemned but it is allowed for health reasons. The use of tobacco and intoxicants is strictly prohibited. Hospitality and sharing food with the hungry and needy is a religious dictate. Dress is not prescribed in the Sikh religion but Sikhs should dress in a simple and modest way. Women should not cover their face. Piercing and tattooing is not allowed. No body hair should be removed. Music has a special place in the Sikh religion as the Sikh Holy Book is written in ragas and the hymns are sung in *kirtan*.

Sikhs are abstained from performing unnecessary rituals. There is no place for superstitions, black magic, pilgrimage, idol worship and Astrology in Sikhism. Sikhs should believe in one God and should not worship many gods and goddesses. The Sikh religion respects other religions and is against fanaticism and forcible conversion. It favours the freedom of speech and worship.

It is important to mention some prominent Sikh denominations and saint preachers namely *Namdharis, Nirankaris, Radhasoamis,* the 3H organisation, *Guru* Nanak *Nishkam Sevak Jatha* which appeared as reform and spiritual movements. These reform movements saved the Sikh religion from decline and made timely contributions by keeping the Sikh religion and religious traditions intact. The saint preachers also spread the message of the *Guru Granth Sahib* far and wide. The contributions of these reform movements and saint preachers were significant. The denominations believing in the principle of a continuous succession and presence of a supreme spiritual authority in a living *guru* distinguished them from mainstream Sikhism. The followers of the saint preachers in many cases found their own unique identities resulting in *gurdwaras* associated with these sects and saints.

Sikhism in a nutshell spread the message of truthful living is higher than truth based on *kirt karo, wand chhako* te *naam japo* (earn with honest and approved means, share with the poor and needy and recite the name of the Creator). God alone is supreme and all humans are God's creation then why discriminate? Love God and care for God's creation. This book reflects Sikh theology through the eyes of the author though there are other religions and faiths. Inderjit expresses his own theological reflections arising out of his own experience of God within his Sikh roots and his Christian way of life. Within that attempt he was able to set up a model for interfaith dialogue when he said "what is needed is for people of different faiths to meet with each other, share experiences of God, and grow in our understanding of God and of each other".

Appendix 1
Contributions of the Sikh Gurus

Sikh *Gurus*

Guru Nanak was the founder of the Sikh religion and he was followed by nine successor *gurus*. This appendix illustrates their contributions to the Sikh faith.

Guru Nanak Dev (1469-1539) was the founder of Sikhism who dedicated himself to the service of humanity. The *Guru* began his mission and preached actively by undertaking a series of journeys between about AD 1499 and 1521. He advocated human dignity and condemned the caste and class system then dominating society. He infused courage and confidence in women who were considered inferior and humiliated. He tried to lift people out of ignorance and superstition. He spread the message that there is only one God and all human beings are God's creation. No one is superior or inferior. Human beings are judged by their actions and not by class and status. One should remember God all the time, earn a living with honest and approved means and share with the needy and the poor. The *Guru* insisted on good moral values. He introduced the practice of praying in a congregation as a family and created *dharamsalas* (places of worship). He spread his message to all irrespective of their religion, caste and class through music. In about AD 1521 he settled in Kartarpur and established the system of the common kitchen.

Guru Angad Dev (1504-1552) was installed as the second *guru* in 1539. *Guru* Nanak nominated one of his disciples as his successor in preference to his sons. The *Guru* was an embodiment of obedience and selfless service. He popularised the *Gurmukhi* script (script used in writing Panjabi, the language used by Sikhs) thereby breaking the monopoly of learning enjoyed by the *Brahmans*, a priestly class. He wrote the life of *Guru* Nanak in prose form in Panjabi based on the information given by Bhai Bala and the other disciples of *Guru* Nanak. The *Guru* also followed and promoted the tradition of *langar* (free kitchen) established by *Guru* Nanak in order to remove caste distinctions and to encourage the concept of *seva* (voluntary service) and sharing therefore strengthening the bonds of union among Sikhs. He set up the discipline for Sikhs and how they should lead their daily life. The *Guru* was known as the healer of incurable diseases. He also composed religious hymns.

Guru Amar Das (1479-1574) became the third *guru* at the age of seventy-three in 1552. He was a devoted disciple of *Guru* Angad and was nominated by the second *guru* as a result of his service and devotion. The *Guru* created twenty-two dioceses, each under the charge of a devout Sikh. He trained one hundred and forty six travelling missionaries who went to different parts of India to preach Sikhism. The *Guru* fixed three festivals for the Sikh congregation i.e. *Diwali, Vaisakhi* and *Maghi* and these gatherings led to greater contact among Sikhs. *Langar* had become a permanent feature by this time and the *Guru's* slogan was '*Pahle pangat: peechhe Sangat*' requiring every visitor to participate in *langar* before meeting him. He raised his voice against evil social practices to undermine women such as the veil, *sati*, infanticide and dowry. He advocated female widow marriage and stressed family life as opposed to renunciation. The *Guru* visualised and made a start of setting up the Sikh centre with a holy pool at a place which has grown into the present city of Amritsar. This project was left to his successor, *Guru* Ram Das to complete.

Guru Ram Das (1534-1581) became the fourth *guru* at the age of forty in 1574. He was the devout son-in-law of *Guru* Amar Das who proved himself worthy of *guruship*. The *Guru* bought land and founded a town which was named as Rampura later known as Amritsar for the residence of Sikhs. He provided facilities for all types of trade so that Sikhs could become self sufficient. The *Guru* also built pools (*sarovars*) and introduced *daswandh* for the humanitarian projects. He was very active in mission work. The *Guru* prescribed the daily routine for Sikhs. The *Guru* simplified the wedding ceremony by endowing it with the sacrament of holy words by writing hymns connected with marriage (*Lavan*). The most outstanding contribution of the *Guru* was the foundation of the city of Amritsar on a land gifted to his wife by King Akbar. The *Guru* made Amritsar the focal point for *Vaisakhi* and *Diwali* gatherings.

Guru Arjan Dev (1563-1606) was the youngest son of *Guru* Ram Das and became the fifth *guru* of the Sikhs at the age of eighteen in 1581. *Guru* Arjan was deeply involved in the early development of Amritsar and helped his father in the supervision of the construction work. The excavation of the holy pool started by his father got completed by the *Guru*. The *Guru* built *Harmandar* (temple of god) *Sahib* now known as the *Golden Temple*, the holiest shrine of the Sikhs. He also built a house for lepers at Tarantaran near Amritsar. The significant contribution made by him was the compilation of *Granth Sahib* which was formally installed at *Harmandar Sahib* in 1604. The *Guru's* relation with the ruling King Jahangir was not cordial and the King ordered his imprisonment on the charges that the *Guru* had helped his son Khushro against him and that he had created communal dissention by compiling *Granth Sahib*. The *Guru* was asked to change certain hymns of *Granth Sahib* to which the *Guru* did not agree. This resulted in severe torture of the *Guru* by pouring boiling water and burning sand over his body and making him sit on a red hot iron plate. He was tortured to death at Lahore in 1606. The life of *Guru* Arjan is an outstanding example of martyrdom for the sake of his faith.

Guru Hargobind (1595-1644) was the only son of *Guru* Arjan dev. He was installed as guru in 1606. The *Guru* knew that the Mughals wanted to weaken the power of the Sikhs so he organised a band of Sikh soldiers. They were trained and armed to challenge the might of the Mughal rulers and to liberate masses from religious and political tyranny. The *Guru* built *Akal takht* opposite to the *Golden Temple*. The *Golden Temple* stands for spiritual guidance and *Akal takht* for dispensing justice and temporal authority. It is from here that the important decisions about the *panth* are made and the *hukamnama* is issued. The *Guru* himself used to carry two swords, one representing the spiritual power (*peeri*) and the other temporal and military power (*meeri*). The *Guru* added a new dimension to Sikhism by introducing the concept of *meeri* and *peeri*. The use of the sword in Sikhism is for purposes of self defence and justice. The Sikhs were transformed from a religious and peaceful group into a martial community. The Mughal King Jahangir got suspicious of the *Guru's* intentions and had him imprisoned in the Gwalior fort for not paying *Jazia* tax (a tax levied on non-Muslims). After two years the *Guru* was ordered to be released but at the insistence of the *Guru* other royal prisoners were also freed. The *Guru* fought four battles against the forces of Emperor Shah Jahan. He was a versatile leader, saint as well as a warrior. He fought to liberate the masses from tyranny and oppression.

Guru Har Rai (1630-1661) got guruship and became the seventh guru at the tender age of fourteen in 1644. He was the grandson of *Guru* Hargobind. He was a man of peace and meditation. He consolidated Sikhism further and taught Sikhs respect for *gurbani*. He appointed disciples to preach in different parts of the country. The *Guru* took a great deal of interest in health care and opened a hospital and dispensary at Kiratpur (Punjab).

Guru Harkrishan (1656-1664) was the younger son of *Guru* Har Rai. He became the eighth *guru* of the Sikhs and assumed the responsibilities of the *guru* at the age of five. The *Guru*, though very young, continued to spread the message of Sikhism and brought about social reforms. He preached against smoking, stealing, gambling, caste system and female infanticide. He lectured to his disciples and healed the sick and looked after the poor. The *Guru* kept busy at Delhi healing the people suffering from a cholera epidemic. He passed away at the age of eight.

Guru Tegh Bahadur (1621-1675) was the youngest son of *Guru* Hargobind, the sixth *guru* of the Sikhs. He was proclaimed *guru* in 1664. He believed that forgiveness is divine and revenge is an evil passion. The *Guru* established a new centre called Anandpur. He also wrote hymns which were added by his son *Guru* Gobind Singh to the *Adi Granth*. He was the champion of religious freedom and protecting the weak. The *Guru* was beheaded in Delhi for protecting the Hindu faith by the orders of the Mughal ruler Aurangzeb. He set a unique example by sacrificing his life against fanaticism and forcible conversion.

Guru Gobind Singh (1666-1708) became the tenth *guru* of the Sikhs in 1675 at a tender age after his father *Guru* Tegh Bahadur was executed by the order of the Mughal emperor Aurangzeb. He knew the challenges ahead and wanted to prepare himself for them. For twenty years, he lived peacefully at Anandpur practicing arms and exercises to complete his training as a soldier. The *Guru* was known as a saint soldier. He created *Khalsa Panth* and transformed the Sikh community into saint soldiers. He started the initiation ceremony and gave Sikhs an identity in the form of the five 'K's. He tried for a casteless and classless society based on universal love. He was a great scholar of Persian and Sanskrit and engaged fifty-two poets. The *Guru* wrote many compositions put together in *Dasam Granth* compiled by *Bhai* Mani Singh after his death. He established a new *gurdwara* at Paunta *Sahib* on the banks of the river Jamuna. He completed the final version of *Granth Sahib* in 1706 by adding the writings of his father. It is believed that he also terminated the line of human gurus by investing the authority in *Granth Sahib* in 1708 before his death. He was a warrior and a natural leader who fought many wars against Mughals and hill *Rajas*. He sacrificed his family and his own life for religious freedom and justice.

Appendix 2
Glossary

Adi	First or original
Adi Granth	Holy Scripture of the Sikhs
Ajuni	Unborn
Akal Purakh	God, not affected by death or time
Akal Takht	a) Supreme Sikh Authority b) A building in the complex of *Golden Temple*, Amritsar
Akhand path	Continuous reading of the *Guru Granth Sahib* taking 48 hours
Amrit	Nectar, solution of water and sugar crystal used at the Sikh ceremony of initiation
Amrit Chhako	To undergo the initiation ceremony
Amritdhari	An initiated Sikh
Anand Karaj	Sikh marriage ceremony
Anandpur *Sahib*	Holy city of Sikhs
Ardas	Sikh prayer recited at the conclusion of a service
Avtara	God in human form
Baba	a) A term used for paternal grandfather b) A term used for a respected and religious man
Bani	Hymns - a term collectively used for the compositions of the *Gurus* and the saints included in the *Guru Granth Sahib*
Baoli	Pool
Barahmaha	Hymns relating to the twelve lunar months

Appendix 2 — Glossary

Betaba	Disclaimer
Bhagat	A devotee
Bhai	a) A term used for a brother b) A respectful term used to address a man c) The custodian of a gurdwara
Bhana Manana	Accepting the Will of God
Bhog	Finishing ceremony of the reciting of *Guru Granth Sahib*
Brahmans	a) Religious caste b) Priests
Burkah	Veil
Chadar	Shawl
Chapati	Flat bread
Chauri	a) Ritual fan made of yak hair waved over the *Guru Granth Sahib* b) Symbol of authority
Chet	Name of Indian lunar month corresponding to March-April
Daaj	Dowry
Dasam Granth	Compositions of the tenth *guru*
Dastar	Turban
Daswandh	Donating one tenth of the earning for religious purposes
Diwali	Festival of lights celebrated by Hindus and Sikhs, which usually falls in the months of October or November
Diwan	A term used for the Sikh act of worship as in Sunday *diwan*
Doli	Departure of the bride from her parent's home

Appendix 2 — Glossary

Ek Oankar	God is one
Five *K's*	Sikh symbols of identity
Ganesh	A Hindu god
Ghar	Denotes musical clef in *gurbani*
Ghund	Face covering
Grace	Favour and kindness
Granth	a) A book b) Literary composition
Granth Sahib	<u>See</u> *Guru Granth Sahib*
Granthi	a) One who looks after the *Granth Sahib* b) A reader of the *Granth Sahib*. c) Custodian of the *Gurdwara*
Gur Maryada/ Guru Maryada	a) According to Sikh religion b) Compulsory rituals in the presence of the *Guru Granth Sahib*
Gurbani	Religious hymns
Gurdwara	a) Literally the house of God or doorway to God b) Sikh place of worship
Gurmat	*Gurus'* teaching
Gurmukhi	Script used for writing Panjabi language
Gurprasad	By the grace of the *Guru*
Gurpurab	Anniversary of the birth or death of Sikh *Gurus*
Gursikh	One who leads his life according to the principles of the Sikh religion
Guru	Religious teacher or a preceptor
Guru Granth Sahib	The Sikh Holy Scripture
Gurughar	Another Panjabi term for a *gurdwara*

Gurumantar	Guru's word
Guruship	To be honoured as a *guru*
Halal	Slaughtered by the process of slow and ritual killing
Halwa	A sweet made of butter, sugar, semolina and dry fruits
Harmandar Sahib	The Golden Temple
Haumen	Individualism or self-centredness
Havan	Holy fire
Hola Mohalla	Sikh festival when mock battles are held by *Nihang* warriors at Anandpur *Sahib*
Holi	Hindu festival held at the full moon in February-March
Hukam	Divine Order
Janamsthan	Birthplace
Jat	Land-owning caste
Jatha	Organisation
Jathedar	A leader of an organisation
Jatheras	Cremation sites of village ancestors
Jazia	Tax levied on non-Muslims by Muslim rulers
Jhatka	Animal killed with one stroke; instantaneously
Jooth	Left over food from one's serving
Jootha	Food touched with used spoons or left over from the tasted or eaten food
Kaccha	Loose fitting underwear - one of the five *K*'s
Kam	Lust
Kangha	Wooden comb - one of the five *K*'s
Kara	Steel bangle - one of the five *K*'s

Karah Prasad	Mixture of semolina, sugar and butter - sacramental food shared at the end of the Sikh service
Karma	Actions/deeds
Karmai	Engagement
Kaur	Name assumed by all female Sikhs - literally it means princess/lioness'
Kes	Uncut hair - one of the five *K*'s
Kesadhari	One who keeps uncut and untrimmed hair and beard
Khalsa	a) The Sikh order, brotherhood instituted by the tenth Sikh guru in 1699 b) The pure ones
Khalsa Panth	Sikh religious order
Khanda	Double-edged sword, one of the emblems of Sikhism
Khatri	A mercantile caste
Kirpan	Sword - one of the five *K*'s
Kirt Karna/ Kirt Karo	Earn a living by honest and approved means
Kirtan	Hymn singing
Krodh	Anger
Kshatriyas	Warrior caste
Kuk	Loud voice
Kukas	Another term used for *Namdharis*
Kurahit	Prohibitions in Sikhism
Lakshmi	Hindu goddess of wealth
Langar	Communal food served in *gurdwaras* free of charge

Lavan	a) Walking around the *Guru Granth Sahib* at the marriage ceremony b) The recitation of four stanzas from the *Guru Granth Sahib* c) Marriage hymns written by the fourth Sikh *guru* Ram Das
Lobh	Greed
Lohri	Harvest festival
Maghi	Harvest and religious festival
Majha	Region in the Punjab
Maryada	Religious tradition
Meeri	Political and military power
Mela	Fair or festival
Mohalla	Denotes the name of the composer *guru* in *gurbani*
Mool Mantra	Fundamental creed (Root Formula)
Mukti	a) Liberation b) Transmigration of the soul and its union with God
Naam	God's name
Naam Japna/ Naam Japo	The reciting of God's name
Naam Laina	Receiving the *guru's* word
Naam Simran	Reciting the name of God
Naamkaran	Naming ceremony
Nagar Kirtan	Religious procession
Namdharis	A Sikh movement founded by *Baba* Ram Singh believe in a living *guru*
Nanakshahi	A Sikh calendar named after *Guru* Nanak
Nirankar	Without form - used for God

Nirankari	A religious sect
Nishan Sahib	Sikh flag, the Sikh emblem
Nishkam Sevak Jatha	a) Organisation of Sikh volunteers b) *Jatha* founded by *Baba* Puran Singh
Pali	Language of Buddhist Scriptures
Palki	Kiosk like seat for the Sikh Holy Scripture
Palla Frowna	Tying the end of the daughter's *dupatta* to the muslin scarf which hangs from the groom's shoulders
Pangat	Sitting together in a row without caste and class distinction
Panj	Five
Panj Pyare	Five beloved Sikhs
Panjabi	The language of the Punjab and also of the Sikh Scripture
Panth	Sikh religious order
Patasha	Sugar crystal
Path	Recitation of the *Granth Sahib* or *gurbani*
Path Bhog	Finishing ceremony
Peeri	Spiritual power
Phagan	An Indian lunar month corresponding to February - March
Pirs	Saints
Pitrs	Ancestors
Prasad	Sacramental food
Punjabi	People of the Punjab
Puranas	Holy Book of Hindus

Puranmasi	Day of full moon
Purdah	Veil
Qur'an	Holy Book of Muslims
Radha	Wife or soul
Radhasoami	A sect which believes in the living *Guru*
Raga	Musical score
Rahit	Sikh identity and Sikh edicts
Rahit Maryada	Sikh Code of Conduct
Rahitnama	Sikh Code of Conduct
Rajas	Kings
Romalla	Expensive cloth to cover the *Guru Granth Sahib*
Saag	Cooked mixed vegetable puree made mainly of green mustard leaves and spinach
Sadharan/Sehaj Path	A non-continuous *path* of the *Granth Sahib*
Sampuran	Complete
Sangat	Congregation
Sangrand	First day of the lunar months
Sant	A pious man/saint
Sant Bhasha	Language used by saints
Sanyas	Renunciation
Sanyasi	One who abstains from worldly comforts and pleasures
Sarbat Da Bhalla	Well being of all
Sargun	a) Endowed with qualities b) Immanent aspect of God

Saropa	Honoured with a *dastar* (turban)
Sarovar	Large pool
Satguru	A true teacher or guide
Sati	Throwing oneself on one's husband's funeral pyre
Satsang	*Kirtan* sessions
Sehajdhari	A Sikh who believes in the teachings of Sikhism but does not keep a Sikh identity
Seva	Voluntary service to the community
Sevadars	Volunteers
Shabad	a) Hymns b) Words of the Holy Book
Shabad Kirtan	Hymn singing
Shradh	Feeding *Brahmans* to honour dead ancestors
Shromani Gurdwara Prabandhak Committee (SGPC)	An authoritative religious committee based in Amritsar, Punjab
Shudras	Caste of menial workers
Sikh Rahit Maryada	The Sikh Code of Conduct
Singh	Literally meaning lion - added as a suffix to the name of Sikh males
Soami	Husband or Lord
Sodhis	One who follows the code of discipline of *Namdharis* only
Takht	Seat of authority
Taksal	Religious school
Talas	a) Musical rhythms b) Musical term to indicate beat

Vaheguru	Wonderful Lord
Vaisakhi	a) The Sikh festival associated with the birth of *Khalsa*. b) Harvest festival
Vaishyas	A trading caste/ traders
Vak	Opening sentence from the left hand page of the *Guru Granth Sahib*
Viakhia	Explaining the religious traditions
Vikrami	Hindu calendar based on lunar calculations
Wand Chhakna/ Wand Chhako	Share with the less fortunate/Sharing with the poor and needy
Word Guru	Refers to *Guru Granth Sahib*
Yogi	a) One who practices Yoga b) A holy person

Bibliography

Adi Granth. See *Sri Guru Granth Sahib*.

Census. Census 2001. Office for National Statistics. London: HMSO. 2003.

Cole, W. O. and Sambhi, P. S. A popular dictionary of Sikhism. Surrey: Curzon. 1990.

Gill, M.K. The role and status of women in Sikhism. Delhi: National Book Shop. 1995.

Gobind Singh *(Guru)*. *Akal Ustat*. In Dasam Granth. Amritsar: Chattar Singh Jiwan Singh. 1998.

Gobind Singh *(Guru)*. *Dasam Granth*. Amritsar: Chattar Singh Jiwan Singh. 1998.

Gopal Singh. *Sri Guru Granth Sahib:* translated and annotated in English. New Delhi: World Sikh Centre. 1984.

Guru Granth Sahib. See *Sri Guru Granth Sahib*

Khokhar, Kulwant Singh. Essays on Sikh values. Amritsar: Chattar Singh Jiwan Singh. 2002.

Kohli, S.S. Sikh ethics. Delhi: Manoharlal. 1975.

Mansukhani, Gobind Singh. The quintessence of Sikhism. 2nd ed. Amritsar: *Shromani Gurdwara Prabandhak Committee*. 1965.

Paramjit Singh. Vaisakhi: Celebrations and Birth of the *Khalsa*. Birmingham: DTF 2003.

Patwant Singh. The Sikhs. London: John Murray. 1999.

Rahi, Hakim Singh. *Sri Guru Granth Sahib* discovered: a reference book of quotations. Delhi: Motilal Banarsi das Publishers. 1999.

Rahit Maryada: A guide to the Sikh way of life. London: 1971. Amritsar: 1978.

Rait, Satwant Kaur. Sikh women in England: Their religious and cultural beliefs and social practices. London: Trentham Books. 2005.

Sahib Singh trans. *Sri Guru Granth Sahib Darpan* (Panjabi). Jallandhar: Raj Publishers.

Sikh Rahit Maryada. Amritsar: *Shromani Gurdwara Prabandhak Committee.* 1992.

Sri Guru Granth Sahib. Amritsar: *Shromani Gurdwara Prabandhak Committee* (Standard verson of 1430 pages in Panjabi).

Teja Singh & Ganda Singh. A short history of the Sikhs. Patiala: Punjabi University. 1989.

Weller, Paul ed. Religions in the UK. Derby: University of Derby, 1997.

All Bible references are to the Revised Standard Version, Oxford University Press 1989.

Index

Ablution	56
Abortion	44, 45, 74
Adi Granth	10, 15, 16, 18, 59, 66
Adultery	7, 44, 55, 74
Ajapal Singh	10
Akal takht	59, 69
Akal Ustat	38
Akhand path	13, 51, 52, 53, 54, 74
Alcohol	10, 12, 13, 56
Amritdhari	1, 48, 60
Amritsar	15, 18, 52, 54, 68, 69
Anand karaj	10, 11, 44, 45, 47, 48, 53, 73
Anand Marriage Act	44
Anandpur Sahib	51, 53, 59
Arabic	16, 19, 72
Ardas	11, 48, 49
Asceticism	23
Ashes	50
Astrology	48, 58, 60, 75
Australia	3
Avtar Bani	11
Avtar Singh (guru)	11
Baba Balak Singh	10
Baba Dayal	11
Baba Puran Singh Kerichowala	13
Baba Ram Singh	10
Banda Bahadur	59
Bangla Sahib	59
Barahmaha	51
Bhai Gurdas	15, 18
Bhai Lalo	33
Bhai Maha singh	53
Bhai Mani Singh	15
Bhaini Sahib	10
Bhajan *Yogi*	12
Bible	66
Birth	8, 18, 21, 22, 24, 31, 34, 38, 47, 50, 53, 59 74
Black magic	75
Brahma	28
Brahmans	31, 50, 54, 58
Brij	16, 19, 72
Canada	3
Canopy	8, 18,
Caste	6, 16, 18, 24, 31, 32, 33, 38, 39, 45, 47, 71, 73, 74
Caste system	7, 10, 11, 14, 16, 31, 34, 39, 42, 45, 71, 74

Index

Celibacy	41, 42
Chamoli	59
Chauri	8, 18
Child marriage	42, 45, 74
Christianity	65, 69
Christmas	69
Civil Marriage Act	44
Classical music	57
Climate change	29, 30, 72
Code of conduct	1, 2, 9, 12, 13, 31, 34, 35, 44, 45, 48, 55, 60, 71, 75
Contraceptive	44, 45, 74
Cremation	49
Daaj	43
Dalit	63
Damdama Sahib	15
Damdamai Taksal	59
Daswandh	5, 6, 10
Death	18, 21, 22, 23, 24, 25, 37, 45, 47, 49, 50, 53, 54, 56, 74
Denominations	3, 9, 14, 75
Devotional music	57
Discrimination	32, 33, 39, 65, 73
Diversity	64,
Divine Order	22, 24
Divorce	44
Diwali	14, 51, 52, 54, 75
Dowry	10, 11, 37, 43, 45, 74
Dress	55, 57, 60, 75
Drugs	10, 12, 56
East Africa	3, 13
Easter	69
Ecology	27, 28, 29, 30, 72
Ecumenism	65
Environment	27, 28, 29, 30, 38, 56, 60, 65, 72
Equality	6, 14, 19, 31, 32, 33, 37, 38, 39, 42, 47, 55, 60, 64, 71, 73, 75
Euthanasia	45
Face covering	37, 57
Family life	7, 14, 23, 34, 36, 41, 45, 48, 53, 55, 60, 71, 73
Family planning	44, 45, 74
Fanaticism	14, 16, 38, 71, 75
Farid	38
Fasting	50, 54, 57, 60, 74, 75
Five articles of faith	4
Five 'K's	2, 13, 14, 52
Folk music	57
Ganesh	52
Gender equality	6, 14, 16, 71, 73

God	3, 5, 6, 7, 11, 13, 14, 15, 17, 19, 21, 22, 23, 24, 27, 28, 29, 30, 31, 32, 33, 36, 38, 41, 44, 45, 47, 49, 54, 55, 57, 58, 59, 60, 61, 62, 63, 64, 65, 66, 67, 68, 69, 70, 71, 72, 74, 75, 76
Goindwal	51
Golden Temple	15, 18, 52, 59, 69
Grace	21, 22, 23, 45, 64, 66, 67, 69
Granthi	8, 36, 47, 49, 50, 51
Gurdwara	4, 5, 6, 7, 8, 9, 13, 14, 18, 29, 30, 33, 47, 48, 49, 50, 51, 52, 53, 54, 56, 59, 60, 61, 73, 74, 76
Gurmaryada/Guru-Maryada	13, 14, 48
Gurmat	1, 2, 55
Gurmukhi	8, 16, 72, 19
Gurpurab	8, 14, 50, 51, 53, 54, 74
Guru Amar Das	16, 22, 28, 29, 32, 36, 37, 41, 42, 51, 61
Guru Angad	16
Guru Arjan Dev	15, 16, 18, 33, 51, 54, 71, 74
Guru Gobind Singh	2, 3, 8, 9, 10. 14, 15, 18, 24, 32, 36, 38, 43, 44, 47, 51, 52, 53, 54, 55, 56, 59, 71, 74, 75
Guru Granth Sahib	1, 8, 10, 11, 13, 14, 15, 17, 18, 22, 24, 25, 31, 33, 34, 35, 38, 39, 42, 44, 45, 47, 48, 49, 51, 53, 54, 55, 56, 59, 71, 72, 73, 74, 76
Guru Hargobind	42, 52, 54, 59
Guru Harkrishan	59
Guru Nanak	2, 5, 15, 16, 17, 21, 22, 27, 28, 31, 33, 34, 35, 50, 51, 54, 57, 58, 61, 71, 74
Guru Nanak Nishkam sevak jatha	13, 75
Guru Ram Das	16, 37
Guru Tegh Bahadur	15, 16, 18, 51, 54, 59, 74
Gwalior Fort	52, 54
Halal	7, 55, 56, 75
Harbhajan Singh Puri	12
Harmandar Sahib	15, 18, 58, 59, 69
Haumen	7, 75
Hemkunt Sahib	59
Hindi	16, 19, 72
Hindvi	16, 19
Hola Mohalla	8, 14, 51, 52, 54, 75
Holi	52, 54
Holika	52
Holy Communion	63
Holy Scripture	15, 18, 21, 24, 27, 29, 33, 36, 45, 55, 57, 71
Homophobia	65
Homosexual relations	45
Hospitality	56, 60, 75
Hukam	6, 28
Idolatry	11, 16, 71
Incarnation	22, 69
Infanticide	10, 34, 36, 37, 44, 45, 73, 74
Initiation	3, 8, 10, 11, 14, 32, 39, 47, 48, 51, 52, 73, 74, 75

Index

Interfaith dialogue	61, 65, 76
Intoxicant	7, 11, 13, 55, 56, 75
Jagatjit Singh	10
Jazia	52
Jesus Christ/Jesus/Christ	62, 63, 64, 65, 66, 67, 68, 69, 70
Jhatka	56, 75
Jooth	56
Jootha	56
Kabir	33, 38
Kachha	3, 4, 14
Kangha	3, 4, 14, 16
Kara	3, 4, 14
Karah Prasad	10
Karma	23, 25, 45, 49
Kes	3, 14
Kesadhari	1
Khalsa	3, 11, 32, 39, 52, 55, 59, 60, 73, 74
Khalsa Panth	7, 32, 39, 51, 54, 73, 75
Khanda	7
Kirpan	3, 4, 14
Kirt karna/kirt karo	4, 5, 23, 76
Kirtan	3, 8, 53, 57, 60, 75
Kirtan Sohilla	49
Kshatriyas	31
Kukas	10
Kurahit	55
Lakshmi	52
Langar	5, 9, 11, 12, 33, 35, 36, 39, 51, 52, 56, 61, 73
Lavan	11, 13, 48, 51
Lesbian and gay marriages	44, 45, 74
Lohri	8, 14, 53, 54
Ludhiana	10
Macrocosm	28
Maghi	8, 14, 51, 53, 54
Maharaja Ranjit Singh	9. 58
Makar Sangrand	53
Malaysia	3
Marriage	34, 36, 41, 42, 43, 45, 47, 48, 53, 73, 74
Mercy killing	45, 74
Mian Mir	58
Microcosmic theory	28
Monogamous marriages	36, 42, 43
Monotheism	21, 22, 24
Mool Mantra	21, 67, 69
Mukatsar	53
Mukti	7
Music	57, 60, 71, 75
Naam	11, 12, 17, 22, 54, 58
Naam japna/ japo	4, 5, 10, 13, 23, 76
Nagar Kirtan	52

Index

Namdharis	10, 75
Naming ceremony	8, 47, 53
Nanakshahi	50, 59
Nankana Sahib	58
New Testament	66
Nirankaris	11, 75
Nishan Sahib	7, 8
Old Testament	66
Palla Frowna	48
Pangat	33, 73 69, 73
Panjabi	9, 13, 16, 19, 61, 72
Path Bhog	50
Patriarchal	34
Persian	16, 19, 72
Pilgrimage	5, 11, 12, 55, 58, 60, 65, 75
Pirs	58
Pitrs	58
Polygamy	7, 34, 36, 74
Prahlad	52
Prakrit	16, 19, 72
Punjab	2, 9, 11, 15, 37, 41, 42, 43, 49, 51, 53
Puranas	38
Puranmasi	50
Purdah	4, 34, 37, 57
Qur'an	38
Racism	65
Radhasoamis	11, 12, 75
Ragas	8, 16, 57, 60, 71, 75
Rahit	2, 13, 55, 75
Ramayan	52
Ravidas	33
Reincarnation	22
Renunciation	7, 14, 41, 45, 73
Romalla	18
Root Formula	21
Sadharan path	13, 50, 51
Samadhis	58
Sangat	8, 11, 35, 43, 52
Sangrand	8, 50, 51, 53, 54, 74
Sanskrit	16, 19, 72
Saropa	4
Sat Sri Akal	59
Sati	34, 36, 37, 73
Sehajdhari	1
Seva	6, 7, 9, 41, 75
Sexism	65
Shabad yoga	12
Shiv Dayal Singh	11
Shiva	28
Shradh	50, 54, 58, 74

Index

Shudras	31
Sikh denominations	3, 9
Sikh ethics	4, 31, 55
Sikh identity	3
Sikh Rahit *Maryada*	1, 9, 37, 42, 55, 56
Sikh symbols	3, 13
Singapore	3
Sis Ganj	59
Smoking	29, 30, 55
Sri Akal Takht	59
Sri Dam Dama Sahib	59
Sri Hazur Sahib	59
Sri Keshgarh Sahib	59
Sri Patna Sahib	59
Suicide	45
Talas	57
Talwandi Sabo	15
The 3H organization	12, 75
Theory of *Karma*	7
Tobacco	10, 55, 56, 75
Transmigration	7, 23, 24, 49
Turban	4, 13
Turban ceremony	50
USA	3
Universe	22, 23, 27, 28, 30, 72
Vaisakhi	8, 14, 51, 52, 54, 74
Vaishshyas	31
Vak	47, 48
Vedas	27
Veil/Veiling	34, 36, 37, 57, 73
Vikrami	51
Vishnu	28
Voluntary service	6, 7, 9, 14, 31, 41, 71
Wand chhakna/chhako	4, 5, 23, 76
Wedding	8, 48, 53, 74
Word *Guru*	8, 17, 67, 71
Zodiac sign	51, 54